NONE OF THE ABOVE

NONE OF THE ABOVE

WHY 2008 IS THE YEAR TO CAST
THE ULTIMATE PROTEST VOTE

JOSEPH FARAH

WND BOOKS

NONE OF THE ABOVE: Why 2008 Is the Year to Cast the Ultimate Protest Vote
A WND Books Book
Published by WND Books, Inc.
Los Angeles, CA

Cover Design by Linda Daly

WND Books books are distributed to the trade by:

Midpoint Trade Books
27 West 20th Street, Suite 1102
New York, NY 10011

WND Books books are available at special discounts for bulk purchases. WND Books also publishes books in electronic formats. For more information call (310) 961-4170 or visit www.wndbooks.com.

First Edition

ISBN: 10-Digit 1935071017
ISBN: 13-Digit 9781935071013
Library of Congress Control Number: 2008931615

Printed in the United States of America

10 9 8 7 6 5 4 3 2 1

TABLE OF CONTENTS

ACKNOWLEDGMENTS

Thank you, Linda Daly, for a great cover. The only difficulty in working with you is that you provide so many great choices in your designs. I have never worked with a finer, more caring, and more passionate artist.

Eric Jackson, chief executive officer of WND Books, deserves credit (some might say "blame") for encouraging me to write this book.

I want to thank Michael Savage for having the courage to endorse this effort, even though he does not necessarily agree with everything written herein. It takes a special kind of media personality and friend to stand by tough ideas. One thing you can say about Michael Savage, he never retreats from ideas that are unconventional, controversial, and outside the box of issues routinely debated and analyzed in what we euphemistically refer to as the "mainstream media."

Without the backing of a spouse on a project like this, it would be a mistake to tackle it. I told Elizabeth about the idea for None of the Above, *and it took all of five minutes for her to jump on board enthusiastically. Thank you, honey. I love your devotion to the causes of truth, justice, and righteousness.*

I accept all of the responsibility for any errors in this book. However, any praise and honor that might accompany it should be directed to my Lord, Savior, and King (the only King that I ever want or accept, by the way) — Yeshua of Nazareth.

INTRODUCTION

THE 2000 PRESIDENTIAL election was the first in which I refused to cast a vote for either major candidate.

Since I had suffered through eight years of a Bill Clinton/Al Gore administration, playing a major part in breaking some of the biggest stories in that scandal-plagued political era, I was not about to pull the lever for Gore.

Indeed, I knew a Gore presidency would have meant disaster for America. I did my best as a journalist to expose him as the big-government zealot he was and remains today.

But it probably surprised more than a few people when I publicly announced I would not—and could not—vote for his rival, Republican challenger George W. Bush.

I vividly remember the day I came to that decision.

It was the very day I met Bush for the first time. It was 1999, and he was Governor Bush and a likely candidate for the presidency the following year.

I learned at that meeting that he was thoroughly clueless and totally unqualified to serve as the president of the United States—destined, if elected, to be an inept leader faithless to the principles of American independence and self-government.

How did I come to this conclusion in just one meeting?

Someone at this private gathering asked the governor of Texas what he would do if a piece of clearly unconstitutional legislation arrived on his desk at the White House.

I will never forget Bush's bone-chilling answer to that question.

"How will I know if it's unconstitutional?" he asked.

Perhaps, since then, Bush has realized that every American—and certainly every elected official—has an obligation to consider the Constitution, a duty to understand it, and the intellectual responsibility to determine whether our laws live up to that founding document of our republic.

Back then, he apparently thought only Supreme Court justices were qualified and empowered to make that determination.

Think about that.

When elected to the presidency, you take an oath to uphold and defend the Constitution of the United States. If you don't understand what that means, how is it possible to execute your oath?

By the way, was I right about Bush?

I think my instincts were correct.

However, in all honesty, the choices put before us this year by the two major parties make George Bush look like George Washington by comparison—especially with regard to our litmus test, the Constitution.

It is principally because of my strong belief in the Constitution that I am urging Americans this year not to vote for either major-party candidate. Neither Barack Obama nor John McCain understands, appreciates, or reveres the charter that serves as the very basis for our unique form of government.

I will address the specifics of that very serious charge later in this book. I will make the case that it is time for a real protest against a broken and corrupt American political system. It's not a time for choosing "the lesser of two evils." That won't fix our country's leadership crisis.

It's time for resistance. It's time for rebellion. It's time for radicalism. It's time to start saying no to the bad choices the system now hands us. It's time to change from a spirit of compliance to government to a spirit of obedience to God and to the Constitution that limits the authority of government.

How does that view translate into the political arena?

For starters, as I wrote in my book *Taking America Back*, moral people—citizens who consider themselves accountable to God first and who uphold the Constitution as the law of the land in America—must oppose any and all politicians who won't strictly adhere to that law. There can be no ifs, ands, or buts about this. You can't vote for the lesser of two evils because that is still voting for evil. It's better not to participate in evil at all.

Admittedly, this is a hard pill for many Americans to swallow. We've been conditioned to believe that voting is our central civic duty. It may be, but not if it means supporting evil—even a shade of evil.

I've been called irresponsible for making that statement. I've been called unrealistic. I've been called impractical. And I've been called worse.

Many Americans have grown convinced they have a sacred obligation to vote—even if it means pulling the lever for an unqualified, hyperambitious dolt who wouldn't know the Constitution if he wiped his feet on it.

You will hear that failure to vote for one of the two major-party candidates in any election is tantamount to "throwing your vote away." I say voting for an illegitimate and unworthy candidate—one who will not live under the rule of law and abide by the Constitution as a minimal standard—is throwing your vote away.

That's exactly what all Americans face in 2008.

Barack Obama and John McCain are unwilling to uphold the Constitution, unqualified to serve as president, and unworthy of our support.

If you don't have a choice you can truly respect, don't vote. Don't *pretend* you have a choice. Don't dignify a corrupt system with your participation in a *charade*. Don't add legitimacy to an illegitimate process.

If you follow my advice, prepare to be criticized. Because too many Americans simply don't understand our unique form of government. They don't understand that we are supposed to be a self-governing people—not a people reliant on government to make our decisions and provide for us. They don't understand that we have a Constitution that sets us apart and strictly limits the power of government, and that if it doesn't mean what it says, we don't have anything special here in America. They don't understand that we are a nation of laws, not of men.

And, most of all, they don't understand that who serves as the president of the United States is simply not all that important in the big scheme of things—especially if the choice is between Tweedle-Dee and Tweedle-Dumber.

Some people—too many, really—think of government and politics every four years. They consider it their sacred duty to vote for either a Democrat or a Republican each presidential cycle, and they believe that to do anything else is a waste of a vote or worse. As long as we continue to choose between two bad options every four years, we will never have a good choice; we will never have better alternatives.

Think about that.

If John McCain becomes the next president of the United States, he will redefine the Republican Party in his own image. He will explain to his party elite that his victory resulted from his "maverick" willingness to "reach across the aisle" and compromise with his political adversaries.

He will explain that political victory means appealing to the mushy middle rather than to the "extremes." And many will listen to him—because he was the architect of victory.

If Barack Obama wins, he, too, will transform his party to an even more radical party—one more in line with the socialist parties of Western Europe than with anything resembling the party of John F. Kennedy.

Our nation is losing many of the attributes that made it great, made it special, made it different. This is far more important to consider than who will be the next president. As Americans, we need to think beyond 2009, 2010, 2011, and 2012.

As long as the two major parties dominate politics in this country, and as long as they both take their constituencies for granted, we will see no improvement in this dire situation.

I believe those who cast votes for McCain or Obama are the ones wasting their votes. We have an opportunity to do something historic in 2008, something important, something revolutionary.

We have a chance to take our country back from these politicians who have no principles, who don't really believe in the American dream, who care more about their own self-empowerment than serving the will of the people and the rule of law.

Sit it out. Protest. Say, "I'm not going to take it anymore." Build a third party that really represents you and your interests and that is committed to the Constitution. Do whatever your conscience dictates, but don't violate your principles and your conscience by voting for either of these unacceptable and unworthy candidates.

When it comes to the Republican and Democratic choices for president this year, I say: "None of the above."

I hope you agree, because this is the *only* choice that can make a positive difference for the future of America.

CHAPTER ONE

THE CORRUPTION OF THE PARTIES

H YSTERIA—"a psychiatric condition variously characterized by emotional excitability, excessive anxiety, sensory and motor disturbances, or the unconscious simulation of organic disorders, such as blindness, deafness, etc."[1]

That's how my dictionary defines "hysteria."

It's a good definition—especially since I use the word to characterize the pathological obsession with the thoroughly unscientific theory that the world is facing doom and gloom from manmade, catastrophic global warming.

For many of the purveyors of this psychosis, there is little reason to offer up facts to counter their delusions. There can be no debate on this matter, they contend. The hour is too late. Perhaps no one expressed this better than "Republican" Governor Arnold Schwarzenegger, who said: "I say the debate is over. We know the science."[2] Anyone who counters their zealotry has suspect motives and is probably on the payroll of the oil industry.

Ironically, of course, the politician most closely associated with global warming hysteria is Al Gore, whose family built its fortune on Occidental Petroleum stock.[3] Now he is attempting to expand his fortune through the sale of carbon credits.[4]

But the real measure of how thoroughly global warming hysteria has pervaded the political culture of America is the fact that President Bush has embraced it. To prove the president's concern about global warming and climate change, in April 2008, the White House proudly issued a fact sheet entitled "Taking Additional Action to Confront Climate Change."

Clear-thinking Americans have nowhere to turn politically to express their skepticism about global warming hysteria.

Barack Obama is an apostle of the cult.

John McCain is an evangelist.

This is tragic because nothing about this religion is true.

- Global warming is not a result of man's activity.

- It cannot be stopped by actions of government or business.

- It is not bad for man or Earth, but good.

- It is part of a cyclical and natural trend of cooling and warming, not a one-way street.

- The slight warming we've witnessed in the last twenty years is not unusual.

- Global warming is not caused by carbon dioxide levels—natural or manmade.

For those reasons and more, the definition of "hysteria" applies to the believers. They get themselves worked up emotionally about nothing. They feel excessive anxiety about nothing. Sensory and motor disturbances disrupt their ability to understand and accept truth on the subject. They are, in effect, rendered blind and deaf to any and all facts, data, and information that might liberate them from their mental disorder.

Send your children to school and they will be indoctrinated into this faith.

Send your young adults to college and they will become missionaries for the faith.

Read your newspaper or watch the network news and you will be a target for conversion or discipleship.

Go to the movies or watch television entertainment shows and you will get old-fashioned, fire-and-brimstone, apocalyptic preaching.

Turn to major-party presidential politics and you will have only the choice of supporting forced global warming tithing on a massive scale.

Criticize the high priests or their proclamations and you face ostracism, ridicule, and excommunication from the new pantheism.

But, just so you don't get the wrong idea, global warming is not really about atonement for mankind's sins against Mother Earth.

Oh, no—not by a long shot.

In fact, this false religion was founded upon the basest materialistic motivations.

It's not about saving the planet. It's not about God or spiritual matters. It's not even about doing good.

Instead, it's about money and power. It's just the latest and most sophisticated effort by elitists to empower themselves at the expense of the people and the rule of law by redistributing wealth as they see fit.

If there is one lesson I want you to take away from this book, it is that politicians don't look out for your best interest. They look out for their own best interest. They want power and they see you as their ticket to power. What they don't tell you is their empowerment generally means your disempowerment— your loss of freedom.

It's not true of all politicians. There are some who genuinely operate within the spirit of American constitutionalism—people who would do nothing to abrogate your freedom knowingly

3

and mean what they say when they swear an oath to uphold the Constitution.

But they are few and far between.

And there are none running for president on a major-party ticket this year.

And there are few notables within the ranks of either the Democratic or the Republican party.

There are reasons to vote "none of the above" in 2008 that transcend the pathetic records and positions of the two major-party candidates.

The American political system has been corrupted over many years in ways that stack the deck against candidates who are qualified and worthy of holding office. Only a revolt—a rejection of business as usual—stands a chance of correcting this trend.

Let me give you an illustration of what I am talking about.

A few years ago, my family took a trip to Philadelphia to tour the historic sites, including the Liberty Bell and Independence Hall. Nearby, a group called the Philadelphia Citizens for Children and Youth was conducting a survey asking, "If I were elected president of the United States, I would..." Participants in the survey got to choose three responses from the answers below:

A. Improve the schools.

B. Make sure the air and water are clean.

C. Protect kids in their homes and in their neighborhoods.

D. Make sure there are lots of after-school programs.

E. Make sure that homeless people are taken care of.

F. Make sure everyone has enough to eat.

G. Make sure that all kids live in safe and sturdy homes.

H. See that there is peace on earth.

I. Make sure that there are lots of parks and other places where kids can be in and learn about nature.

J. Help parents learn how to care for their kids.

4

That's it. That was the totality of the survey. Those were the choices. These answers were the only possibilities offered in the survey for the priorities of the *executive branch of the federal government.*

What's wrong with those choices?

I'm afraid too many Americans wouldn't recognize the insidiousness of such a survey. We've been dumbed down by a thoroughly corrupt government-run education system whose central goal seems to be to make us all compliant subjects rather than moral, intelligent, self-governing individuals.

The purpose of this survey is obvious. It is the essence of what is taught in schools about civic responsibilities. It is the essence of the political messages of our popular culture. It is the essence of what our key cultural institutions teach us about the role of government in our lives.

Yet, it is the very antithesis of what America's founding documents tell us about the limits of governmental power and authority over our lives.

There is a concerted effort to persuade Americans that government—especially the federal government—has the power and duty to intervene in the lives of individual citizens at every level in every conceivable way. It is nothing short of a plot to convince us all that our wildest dreams will come true if only we put our faith in government—the key to solving any and all imaginable problems.

I can think of no more dangerous idea we could teach our kids. And this happened in Independence Hall—the historic site commemorating our nation's fight for individual freedom, national sovereignty, and self-governance—simply adding insult to injury.

Even more dangerous is the fact that both parties in Washington buy into the concept—in action, if not in rhetoric—that the fundamental answers to our societal problems can be found in deeper federal involvement in schools and increased spending on programs that could never work even if they were constitutional.

Obviously, the presidency was never designed for such purposes. The federal government was never meant to be involved in every facet of our lives. That is the urgent lesson we should be teaching our kids. We should be teaching them the uniquely American principles of self-reliance, personal responsibility, and vigilance against tyranny.

The only things elected officials in Washington could do to solve the problems named in this survey would be to disengage from them—to admit that central control is a mistake, one forbidden by our Constitution.

What legitimate role does the federal government have in schools?

None. That's what the Constitution says. Education is a personal, family matter. If parents want to get together and build schools and cooperative education programs for their children, that's great. But please don't reach into the pockets of people who may have starkly different ideas about what they would teach. Don't force people in other communities and other states to subsidize the schooling of your kids.

How can the federal government help to clean up air and water?

One of the best ways would be for the federal government to sell off millions of acres of land accumulated by Washington over the last two hundred years and to restore the constitutional commitment to private property. The fact is that people are generally much better stewards of their own property than government is. And government should stop lying to the American people about phantom environmental "crises" like "global warming" and "man-made, catastrophic climate change."

How can the federal government protect kids in their homes?

It could make a start by repealing all unconstitutionally approved legislation restricting the right to bear arms, so that parents, whose business *is* the protection of children in their homes, would have the tools they need to do so. The federal government also has the responsibility to promote civil defense, to minimize the death and destruction planned by terrorists and other enemies who seek to kill as many Americans as possible in the coming years. Of course, civil defense is not even on the federal government's radar screen.

What about after-school programs?

Congress should eliminate the income tax, so that mothers could afford to return to the home and provide the best kind of after-school programs for their kids—loving home care.

How about taking care of the homeless?

The solutions for even the most destitute Americans are not to be found in Washington. They are to be found in homes, in churches, in community organizations—where special, individual care can be provided to people in need. Throwing money at problems like this only exacerbates them, as history proves. That's why you will find nothing in the Constitution suggesting a role for the federal government in meeting the needs of individual Americans. The federal government is only authorized and empowered to promote the "general welfare"—not to rob Peter to pay Paul.

How about making sure everyone has enough to eat?

Maybe the federal government needs to stop providing those unconstitutional agricultural subsidies that pay farmers not to grow food. And maybe the elimination of the unconstitutional death tax would permit family farms to remain family farms. Everyone should have enough to eat. But depending on the federal government to make that happen is merely passing the buck to a bureaucracy that will only make problems worse.

How about safe and sturdy homes?

A good start in this direction would be the condemnation of all those federal government housing projects that are little more than death traps and prisons for people seduced into perpetual dependency by Washington.

Peace on earth?

That's something I pray for night and day—and I encourage other Americans to do the same. But the federal government's job is to protect the people of the United States. Peace through strength has served us well when we have applied the principle.

Parks and nature?

Has anyone noticed that most of the severely restricted parkland in the United States is controlled by the federal government? Indeed, something needs to be done about that. Let the kids and their parents have access to the land for which they paid.

How about helping parents learn how to care for their kids?

Wow. That is scary. That many Americans actually think this is a proper role for the president or the federal government illustrates just how far our nation has descended into constitutional illiteracy. The government is a fearsome nanny—as we are about to learn when one of the two nanny-state candidates running for president takes power in 2009.

There are no utopian solutions to any of these problems. But we are conditioning parents and children to believe there are. Why? Because it empowers politicians and restricts freedom—and there is always an elite corps of impudent snobs who seek to do just that.

What are the objectives of government education today? Have you ever wondered? Have you ever asked yourself? Have you ever asked the National Education Association (NEA), which wields so much power over schools and politicians in the United States?

You won't like the answer: Bilingual education. Gay, lesbian, and transgender education. Environmental education. After-school care. Before-school care. Condoms. Self-esteem. And worse.

What is education supposed to be about? It might help if thinking American people (those whose minds have not been thoroughly co-opted by the government propaganda mills) got a little reminder.

Here's how Thomas Jefferson (Do you remember that name, Americans?) described education objectives in 1818—long before the NEA came on the scene:

1) *To give to every citizen the information he needs for the transaction of his own business.*

2) *To enable him to calculate for himself, and to express and preserve his ideas, his contracts and accounts, in writing.*

3) *To improve, by reading, his morals and faculties.*

4) *To understand his duties to his neighbors and country, and to discharge with competence the functions confided to him by either.*

5) *To know his rights; to exercise with order and justice those he retains; to choose with discretion the fiduciary of those he delegates; and to notice their conduct with diligence, with candor, and judgment.*

6) *And, in general, to observe with intelligence and faithfulness all the social relations under which he shall be placed.*[5]

Do you think those goals stand up? Do you think they jibe with the NEA political agenda? Do you think the federal Department of Education would concur?

Or, do you—like me—wonder whether they would even understand what Jefferson was talking about?

There's a bold new political and cultural push in America to make everyone dependent on government.

You don't need guns to defend yourself and your family. Just call 911.

You don't need to prepare for disasters. Just call 911.

You don't need to worry about paying for healthcare yourself. Just call 911.

There isn't anything government can't do for you.

That's what we're being told.

We're all going to live in a brand new utopian world, according to the swirling rhetoric of Barack Obama and his party. McCain and his party, on the other hand, don't explain what's wrong with this approach. Instead, they try to sell the American people lower expectations—rather than freedom.

One way or another, we'll just tax the rich, then the rest of us will be on Easy Street. All our basic needs will be met. We'll live in a just and fair society.

It's amazing so many people actually believe this stuff, especially after social experiments like this have failed miserably over the last century—resulting in massive suffering and deaths numbered in the hundreds of millions.

But believe they do.

I'm not sure there's any way to reason with people who are intellectually dysfunctional—whose own greed and envy motivate them to resemble the French revolutionaries far more than our own American revolutionaries.

Having said that, let's try a little shock treatment.

Let's see what happens in real life when they are dependent on government—totally dependent.

Earlier this year, Brenda Orr of Doylestown, Pennsylvania, a multiple sclerosis victim, placed a 911 call when she became engulfed in fire.

Remember, Brenda didn't have a choice about relying on government. You still do.

Panicked by the flames, she did what Americans have become conditioned to do in any emergency—call 911.

Even though ten dispatchers and four supervisors were on duty and no other calls were coming into the emergency center, a county government operation, no one answered the call for twenty-eight seconds.

Then Brenda was immediately put on hold—despite her pleas.

Another twenty-six seconds passed before a second dispatcher put down his coffee and picked up the phone.

When you listen to the audio recording of the 911 call, you can hear the torment and frustration in Brenda's incredulous voice as she speaks her final words about thirty seconds later.

While that phone rang six times, there were ten people on duty able to answer it. They all failed to do so. Their watercooler chitchat or their Internet surfing was more important to them.[6]

Here is what is even more shocking: *none of the dispatchers or their bosses was fired*.[7] That's the way government protects its own. This is the reason people love government jobs. Government employees are really the only ones protected by government.

This horror story is a metaphor for dependency on government—whether it is for your medical care, whether it is for your family's safety, or whether it is for the way you renew your driver's license.

The reason no one was seriously disciplined in the emergency center is that this kind of service is not unusual—not in Doylestown or anywhere else across America, especially in major urban centers. You've probably experienced something similar—hopefully while in less dire circumstances than those Brenda Orr faced.

Dependency on government is the opposite of freedom and responsibility. In the long term, it means tyranny and slavery. It inevitably slides into massive death tolls, as it did under Mao, Hitler, Stalin, Pol Pot, et al.

I didn't know Brenda Orr. But I hope and pray her death is not in vain. I don't just mean that the people of Doylestown, Pennsylvania, will get better emergency service in the future. Rather, I hope her story wakes up Americans to the reality of what dependency on government really signifies.

Where are the politicians today promoting self-reliance, personal responsibility, and self-government? Where are the politicians committed in their hearts, souls, and minds to the constitutional principle of limited government and enumerated powers?

There are none running for president this year—at least, not as the nominee of one of the two major parties.

So don't vote for either one. It's just that simple. To vote for either John McCain or Barack Obama would be a betrayal—by you—of the Constitution.

Say no. Say "none of the above." Vote third party. Write in your favorite candidate.

I am not, by the way, advocating staying home from the polls this year. I am advocating using real discernment and judgment. I am telling you not to be one of the lemmings who charge off the cliff because everyone else is going in that direction. I am saying it's time to send a big message to Washington and to the party elites that you're not going to take it anymore.

Again, it's not just a problem with McCain and Obama. The two major parties holding a hammerlock of control over government in America represent institutional problems. At least one of them—preferably both—needs to be redeemed. The only alternative is to raise up a viable new party committed to the founding principles that made America great.

Don't let anyone tell you that it's not possible. Don't believe the experts. Don't listen to the political gurus who would convince you to keep playing the same old game—even though the results are rigged.

Just look at what the experts told you at the beginning of this presidential campaign.

We were told early on Hillary Clinton had the Democratic nomination all wrapped up—even before a single vote was cast.

We were told the only guy who could beat her was Rudy Giuliani, and he was virtually anointed as the GOP nominee by some pretty powerful talk radio hosts and analysts.

Later, we were told Fred Thompson would sweep into the race late and immediately become a contender.

Then some suggested Mitt Romney was the only choice, the only candidate who could beat Hillary or Obama or whomever the Democratic nominee might be. Even more important, they said he was the only guy who could deny the dreaded John McCain the Republican nomination.

Some of these powerful voices are friends of mine. I generally respect them. I expect a lot from them—including being right most of the time.

The lesson? So far, the experts have been 100 percent. They've been wrong every time.

In other words, they don't know any more than you or me.

So, do your homework. Vote your convictions, not the lowest common denominator.

There's plenty at stake.

This year, America celebrates its 232nd year of independence. We celebrate our independence every July 4. But the holiday is not "the Fourth of July," as we often call it. It's not just the day we shoot off Chinese-made fireworks. It's not just the day we barbecue burgers. It's not just the day we go to the beach. It's Independence Day—so named because on or about this date in 1776, a group of courageous men risked their lives, their fortunes, and their sacred honor for a dream of freedom and sweet autonomy from an imperial power.

By the way, it wasn't just the birth of American freedom. It was the birth of freedom around the world. That's why the French called George Washington not just the Founding Father of the American Revolution, but "the father of freedom." He was truly the inspiration for freedom fighters everywhere.

Unfortunately, too few Americans today put much value in independence. Most no longer celebrate, cherish, or appreciate independence. Independence is not considered an ideal.

Our political and cultural elite don't want to see a nation full of independent-minded, self-governing citizens who will hold their leaders accountable to the citizens' will and to the laws of the land. They prefer sheep. So they conspire to bring into America millions and millions more sheep.

You will hear the elite preach about the value of living in an "interdependent" world. Have you heard that? "Interdependence"—this is considered a good thing. Keep in mind every time you hear the word "interdependence" glorified and revered that "interdependence" is simply a synonym for "dependence."

It has nothing to do with "independence"—that thing for which our founders risked their lives, their fortunes, and their sacred honor.

The sad truth is the American dream of independence has been betrayed. Americans are worse off today, in terms of individual freedom, than they were before the War of Independence. In fact, take a look at the dictionary definition of "colony" and see if it doesn't apply to us today:

> **Colony:** 1) a group of people who settle in a distant land but remain under the political jurisdiction of their native land; 2) a territory distant from the state having jurisdiction or control over it.[8]

Aren't Americans, in a sense, all colonists of the great imperial throne in the District of Columbia? We all pay tribute to this faraway empire. We are, in reality, little more than serfs doing the bidding of those in the federal corridors of power in Washington. We're taxed without real representation. We're forced to support a growing standing army of federal police in our communities. And we face a growing threat of disarmament—one of the great fears of the colonists who touched off the American Revolution at Lexington and Concord.

What do you think?

Are we better off today that our forefathers were in 1776?

Are we living freer lives today than did the founders?

If George Washington and Thomas Jefferson could return today to see America—the tax rates, the overreaching central government, the subservience of the states to Washington, the non-limitations on the federal government—would they consider us free? Would they consider us independent?

Is American sovereignty and independence still worth a fight?

What are you willing to risk? What are you willing to sacrifice today in the name of freedom and independence?

I'm telling you, 2008 is a critical election year. Settling for the "lesser of two evils" means you will never recover those principles—never rediscover your lost freedoms; never have vibrant and lively and meaningful political debates; never be permitted to be the kind of sovereign, independent, self-governing individual our founding documents promise you the opportunity to be.

I'm not ready to give up on that dream.

I hope you will join me this year in a historic act of defiance.

CHAPTER TWO

OBAMA—UN-AMERICAN AND UNQUALIFIED

W E'VE GOT to get the job done there, and that requires us to have enough troops so that we are not just air-raiding villages and killing civilians, which is causing enormous pressure there."[1]

Sen. Barack Obama said it.

No, it wasn't a harsh indictment of American foreign policy in Vietnam made during his college days.

It wasn't even tough rhetoric he employed to illustrate his contention that we are losing the war in Iraq.

This was Obama's view of what the U.S. military is doing today in Afghanistan.

You might think a major U.S. presidential candidate who made such an ill-advised statement for the entire world to hear would be drummed right out of the race.

You would be wrong.

One of the reasons he has survived the fallout from this gaffe—and dozens of others like it—is because the largest news-gathering agency in the world came to his defense.

"A check of the facts shows that Western forces have been killing civilians at a faster rate than the insurgents have been killing civilians," wrote Associated Press staffer Nedra Pickler in what was released as a "fact check" article on August 14, 2007.[2]

It continued: "The U.S. and NATO say they don't have civilian casualty figures, but the Associated Press has been keeping count based on figures from Afghan and international officials. Tracking civilian deaths is a difficult task because they often occur in remote and dangerous areas that are difficult to reach and verify."

The AP went on to suggest al-Qaida and Taliban terrorists, whom the news agency euphemistically called "militants," had killed 231 civilians in 2007, while Western forces had killed 286.

There you go! Same difference, right? Talk about comparing apples and oranges!

Nowhere in Obama's shameful quote or in the context surrounding it did he compare the numbers of civilian deaths caused by Western forces and those inflicted by al-Qaida and Taliban terrorists. He was, in fact, making the point that more U.S. ground troops are needed to avoid the practice of *deliberately* targeting villages from the air.

So what, I have to ask, is the relevance of this so-called fact check? It has nothing to do with the point being made by Obama.

If there were any validity to Obama's assertion that the United States was deliberately "air-raiding villages" with the intent of killing civilians, doesn't it stand to reason there would be more than 286 civilian deaths in 2007? If the U.S. policy objective was to maximize the civilian death toll, I would have to conclude it is not a model of efficiency.

Remember, we attacked the Taliban and al-Qaida in Afghanistan because they cooperated in a one-day air raid on the United States that killed nearly three thousand civilians!

I was shocked when I heard Obama utter these words. I shouldn't have been, knowing his woeful inexperience in politics generally and in foreign affairs specifically.

What was more shocking to me as a newsman of thirty years' experience was the quick excuse-making and rationalizations offered by the world's largest news-gathering agency, the one that feeds information to thousands of newspapers, Web sites, and radio stations and thus has more influence than the *New York Times*, CNN, ABC, NBC, and CBS combined.

But, then again, none of those news organizations saw anything strangely un-American about this statement by a leading candidate for the presidency of the United States.

There was more to come from Barack Obama—even though the establishment press has tried to put the best face on his rhetoric.

Take the case of what happened when U.S. District Judge James Munley, an appointee of Bill Clinton, overturned an ordinance passed overwhelmingly by the citizens of a small town in Pennsylvania to prohibit renting to those in the United States illegally.

Barack Obama called it "a victory for all Americans."[3]

The heroic mayor of Hazelton, Louis J. Barletta, fulfills his promise to his constituents by enacting an ordinance last summer prohibiting renting to those in the United States illegally. A group of "activists" challenges the law in court. And a federal judge overturns the popular measure with a stroke of the pen.

That is what Barack Obama characterizes as "a victory for all Americans."

A victory for those who no longer believe in the rule of law, perhaps.

A victory for those who no longer believe in the will of the people, perhaps.

A victory for illegal aliens, perhaps.

A victory for Americans who don't mind being ruled by oligarchs and unaccountable judges, perhaps.

But "a victory for all Americans"?

How does he figure?

"The anti-immigrant law passed by Mayor Barletta was unconstitutional and unworkable—and it underscores the need for comprehensive immigration reform so local communities do not continue to take matters into their own hands," explains Obama.[4]

Oh, I see his point.

How dare local officials pass local laws?

How dare local officials defy the elite view?

In fact, why bother to have local elections at all?

Let's just let the courts and the federal government rule over one and all. Is that what we can expect from a Barack Obama presidency? Apparently so.

Obama's solution is simple. Just ram that amnesty plan down the throats of all Americans whether we like it or not.

"Recently, the U.S. Senate failed the American people by blocking progress on immigration reform for the second time in two years," he said. "We cannot put this off any longer. The ongoing problems with our immigration system are dividing our country, and distracting us from the work we need to do in other important areas such as healthcare, education, and jobs."[5]

This man is a demagogue. What's even more bizarre is that statements of this kind don't seem to raise much attention. They don't seem to get the analysis they deserve. They don't seem to get the scrutiny they warrant. My guess is you have never read this quote until today.

Does anyone else realize what he's saying?

People can vote, as long as they vote "correctly."

Local governments can govern, as long as they govern "correctly."

Legislators can legislate, as long as they legislate "correctly."

The biggest victories for the people come when judges overrule the will of the people.

The biggest victories for the people come when the state imposes its will on the people.

The biggest victories for the people come when Barack Obama's political agenda wins at any cost.

I'm old enough to remember this kind of euphemistic "victory for the people." It was a common occurrence—in the days of the old Soviet Union.

And maybe that's the kind of government Barack Obama would like to see for America.

It turns out Barack Obama was, in fact, mentored by a very active member of the Communist Party USA while living in Hawaii and Chicago. Cliff Kincaid, of Accuracy in Media, and Herbert Romerstein, a former investigator with the U.S. House Committee on Un-American Activities, put together reports on Obama's association with Frank Marshall Davis, an African American poet and journalist who was also a CPUSA member. The CPUSA was, at the time, controlled and funded by the Soviet Union.

In a paper titled "Communism in Hawaii and the Obama Connection," the authors document that in 1948, Davis decided to move from Chicago to Honolulu at the suggestion of what they describe as two "secret CPUSA members," actor Paul Robeson and Harry Bridges, the head of the International Longshoremen's and Warehousemen's Union, or ILWU.[6]

In his autobiography, *Dreams from My Father*, Obama discusses the influence a mentor identified in the book only as "Frank" had on his intellectual development.

Obama describes Frank as a drinking companion of his grandfather, who had boasted of his association with African American authors Richard Wright and Langston Hughes during the time Frank was a journalist in Chicago.

In a second report, "Communism in Chicago and the Obama Connection," Kincaid and Romerstein present evidence supporting their contention that the Students for a Democratic Society organization, from which the Weather Underground organization and radicals Bill Ayers and Bernardine Dohrn came, received financial contributions from the CPUSA, which in turn received its funding from Moscow.[7]

Obama's run for the Illinois State Senate was launched by a fundraiser organized at the Chicago home of Ayers and Dohrn by Alice Palmer. Palmer had named Obama to succeed her in the State Senate in 1995, when she decided to run for a U.S. congressional seat.

Nine years before Palmer picked Obama to be her successor, she was the only African American "journalist" to travel to the Soviet Union to attend the 27th Congress of the Communist Party of the Soviet Union, according to an article published in the CPUSA newspaper, *People's Weekly World*, on June 19, 1986.[8]

According to Kincaid and Romerstein, U.S. Peace Council executive committee member Frank Chapman "blew the whistle on communist support for Obama's presidential bid and his real agenda" in a letter to the *People's Weekly World* after Obama's win in the Iowa Democratic Party caucuses. "Obama's victory was more than a progressive move; it was a dialectical leap ushering in a qualitatively new era of struggle," Chapman wrote. "Marx once compared revolutionary struggle with the work of the mole, who sometimes burrows so far beneath the ground that he leaves no trace of his movement on the surface."[9]

Kincaid and Romerstein wrote, "The clear implication of Chapman's letter is that Obama himself, or some of his Marxist supporters, are acting like moles in the political process. The suggestion is that something is being hidden from the public."[10]

There is no overstating the enthusiasm of the old hard-line Communists for the candidacy of Barack Obama in 2008. A survey of the official CPUSA newspaper shows it is pulling out all the stops for Obama. The little red rag can't even disguise its giddiness about the junior senator from Illinois.

So what's the takeaway? What does this mean to real Americans—the hundreds of millions of us who don't read the *People's Weekly World*?

It means Obama is more radical, more revolutionary, more socialist, more communist in his worldview than even Hillary. He is more radical, more revolutionary, more socialist, and, yes, more communist in his worldview than any previous major-party nominee for the U.S. presidency in the history of our country.

Keep in mind, these are ideologues who don't make rash decisions. They don't jump on bandwagons. They make calculated and well-considered choices based on one thing—who comes closer to representing the highest ideals of the *Communist Manifesto* and Marxist-Leninism.

These are Stalinists, stuck in another era, unable to see the world as it really is because of their delusional pathology that leads them down the deadly, oppressive path of totalitarianism.

They looked hard into the faces of Hillary and Obama. They studied their records. They pored over their position papers. And they—the U.S. version of a politburo—determined Barack Obama is their man.

When the Communist Party gets behind a candidate, it's not just words in a newspaper. The party dispatches *apparatchiks* to work hard for the candidate. It occurs to me we may very well have seen a couple of those workers of the world inside Obama's Houston office—those ladies flying the Cuban flags emblazoned with images of Ernesto "Che" Guevara.[11]

What did Obama have to say about those flags?

He didn't insist they come down.

He didn't denounce them as insensitive or sickening or an emblem of evil.

He simply dismissed them as "inappropriate."[12]

Inappropriate?

"Inappropriate" is when somebody tells an off-color joke.

"Inappropriate" is when a campaign worker passes gas in the office.

Displaying an image of Che Guevara as if he were some kind of Third World hero is an abomination. Check that. It's an "Obama-nation."

Who was Guevara? Let's review.

Guevara was born in Argentina in 1928 and originally trained to become a doctor at the University of Buenos Aires. In 1952, he embarked on the trip across South America dramatized in *The Motorcycle Diaries*. After returning to

Buenos Aires to complete his medical degree, Guevara set off again to travel through the Americas. He participated in leftist movements in Guatemala and Mexico and became acquainted with Cuban expatriates in those countries. He joined Castro's revolutionary Cuban army in 1956 as a top commander and Castro's personal physician. He helped Castro topple the regime in Havana in 1959.

As Castro's right-hand man in the new regime, Guevara ordered the execution of hundreds of people while in charge of the notorious La Cabaña, a prison in Havana. He was unapologetic about the mass killings of innocent people, explaining, "To send men to the firing squad, judicial proof is unnecessary. These procedures are an archaic bourgeois detail. This is a revolution! And a revolutionary must become a cold killing machine motivated by pure hate."

Pure hate. It wasn't the first time Guevara used the expression, nor the last. He explained how it must be a tool in the arsenal of revolutionary terrorists—permitting them to do things they would otherwise never be able to accomplish.

"Hatred as an element of struggle; unbending hatred for the enemy, which pushes a human being beyond his natural limitations, making him into an effective, violent, selective and cold-blooded killing machine—this is what our soldiers must become," Guevara said.

During the Cuban Missile Crisis, Guevara was in favor of a nuclear war with the United States because he believed that a better world could be built from the ashes, regardless of the cost in millions of lives. He was overruled by cooler heads in the Kremlin and in Cuba. The nuclear missiles headed for Cuba, ninety miles from the United States, were returned to Russia.

Disgraced by the slight, Guevara went on to create new revolutionary movements and wage armed struggle in Africa and Latin America. He was killed in the jungles of Bolivia in 1967.

Guevara was proud of the fact that he personally put bullets in the backs of the heads of many he considered counterrevolutionary.

Once again, in rallying his guerrillas in Angola, he wrote: "Blind hate against the enemy creates a forceful impulse that cracks the boundaries of natural human limitations, transforming the soldier into an effective, selective and cold killing machine. A people without hate cannot triumph against the adversary."

Would you say displaying this man's picture is "inappropriate"? I'd say that's the biggest understatement since Gen. George Custer said, "Over that hill, I think they're friendly Indians."

Are you starting to put this together? Are you seeing Barack Obama for the extremist he is?[13]

Think about this now.

This guy could actually become the president of the United States.

If he does, it won't be like the Manchurian Candidate backing into the highest office in the land. If Barack Obama wins the White House, the Communists will have gotten their man in the conventional way—through an actual election, working through the system.

Now let's take a look at Mr. and Mrs. William Ayers—referred to briefly earlier in this chapter.

Does Barack Obama have some explaining to do about accepting money from two unrepentant, homegrown, communist revolutionary terrorists who bombed the Capitol, the Pentagon, police stations, and banks in the 1970s?

Yes, I think he does. But there's a much bigger question raised by Obama's relationship with William Ayers and his wife, Bernardine Dohrn, ringleaders of the Weather Underground organization. The question is, why is a couple like this not only accepted in liberal Democratic Party circles and the academic world, but embraced with open arms—in fact, rewarded for their self-declared armed struggle against America, a war they still defend adamantly to this day?

That is a question that, if answered, would explain the way the Democratic Party today is a covert tool of political manipulation whose core agenda is to transform America into the kind of "socialist workers' paradise" envisioned by these one-time violent revolutionaries who were forced to change tactics but not their goals. But more on that in the next chapter.

Let's take a look at whom Dohrn and Ayers really were—and really are:

- Both went underground after she was charged with instigating riots at the Democratic National Convention in Chicago in 1968 and after several of their fellow Weatherman associates were killed when bombs they were building blew up in a Greenwich Village townhouse. One of those killed was Ayers's girlfriend at the time, Diana Oughton. The group was planning to bomb Fort Dix Army Base in New Jersey.[14]

- Dohrn publicly celebrated the group's maiming of Chicago prosecutor Richard Elrod in the Chicago riots. In 1970, rich kid Ayers, son of the chairman of Commonwealth Edison, explained what the Weather Underground was all about: "Kill all the rich people. Break up their cars and apartments. Bring the revolution home, kill your parents, that's where it's really at."[15]

- Following the mass murders of actress Sharon Tate and others by disciples of Charles Manson, Dohrn had this to say: "Dig it. First they killed those pigs, then they ate dinner in the same room with them, then they even shoved a fork into a victim's stomach! Wild!"

Dohrn went on to suggest adopting a "fork salute" might be appropriate for her fellow homicidal maniacs.[16]

- Dohrn, along with other members of the Weather Underground, traveled to Cuba to meet with representatives of the Communist North Vietnamese and Cuban governments as the Vietnam War raged.

- Dohrn was signatory to the Weather Underground's "Declaration of State of War" against the U.S. government. Besides being the pinup girl of the domestic terrorist group, she also co-authored its manifesto, *Prairie Fire*, and helped make the organization's covertly filmed propaganda documentary.

- Ayers participated in more than thirty bombings during his eleven-year reign of underground terror. He says his only regret is not doing more to "bring the war home" to America. In an interview published in the *New York Times*, ironically dated September 11, 2001, he said: "I don't regret setting bombs. I feel we didn't do enough."[17]

- Ayers and Dohrn surfaced in 1980 and turned themselves in to face the riot charges. The federal charges were dropped because the FBI used illegal wiretaps to learn of their crimes. Only a local charge of aggravated assault stuck to Dohrn. She pleaded guilty to two counts, receiving a $1,500 fine and no jail time.[18]

- However, their New York gang continued robbing banks and conducting armed holdups. In 1981, a robbery in Rockland County left a

Brinks security guard and two police officers dead. Dohrn and Ayers refused to cooperate with the investigation of the crime. The woman now teaching law explained she did not believe grand juries were legal. She even refused to provide a signature for handwriting analysts in the case. She was held in contempt and imprisoned for seven months.[19]

- Dohrn served as manager of Broadway Baby, a chic children's boutique in Manhattan's Upper West Side, that served as a money-laundering center and a ring for ID theft. IDs used by participants to rent a getaway car in the Brinks robbery were stolen from customers at Broadway Baby.

- Ayers and Dohrn married while on the lam.

Now, suppose you or your children had a record like that. What kind of future would you expect? Would you imagine that following a brief period of quiet rehabilitation, you would be welcomed into tenured and comfortable positions in academia? Do you think you would get a chance to work with powerful politicians? Do you think you would have the opportunity to decide how hundreds of millions of dollars would be given away by a major philanthropic foundation?

That's exactly what happened to this pair of degenerates.

Today, Ayers teaches at the University of Illinois and works on "school reform" issues—which probably means designing ways to indoctrinate your children into his diseased, evil mindset. In 1999, he joined the Woods Fund of Chicago, where he served as a director alongside Barack Obama until the latter left in 2002. Ayers went on to become Woods's chairman of the board, overseeing the distribution of about $60 million a year. In 2002, the Woods Fund made a grant to

Northwestern University School of Law's Children and Family
Justice Center, where, coincidentally, his wife works.

Dohrn teaches law at Northwestern University and specializes
in "juvenile justice reform"—which suggests she wants your kids
to live out her undying dream of chaos in America's streets and
communities. She still runs the Children and Family Justice
Center. She also sits on boards of the American Civil Liberties
Union and the American Bar Association.

It's worth noting that Ayers's father, Thomas, who stood by
his son throughout his eleven-year run as a fugitive, was a
trustee at Northwestern University and former board chairman.

Who says privilege doesn't have its perks?

Who says crime doesn't pay?

Who says the penalty for treason is death?

Is it important that Obama's political career was essentially
launched in the living room of William Ayers and Bernardine
Dohrn? Yes, it's important. But there are much bigger questions
raised by this story.

Hillary Clinton would like you to believe Obama's
relationship with these domestic terrorists is unusual in
Democratic Party circles.

She said: "And what they [Weather Underground] did was
set bombs and in some instances people died. I know Sen.
Obama is a good man and I respect him greatly, but I think this
is an issue that certainly the Republicans will be raising."[20]

In other words, to Hillary, the only importance to this
relationship is that it might be exploited by Republicans.

That's understandable coming from her, because Hillary's
record is not exactly sinless in regard to support for domestic
terrorists like Ayers and Dohrn.

As president, Hillary's husband commuted the prison
sentences of two other Weather Underground members and of
Puerto Rican terrorists also convicted of bombing the Capitol.

No word yet on the academic appointments Hillary's
terrorists have received.

Why is it that Democrats embrace the likes of this scum?

Why are vermin like Ayers and Dohrn and Hillary's terrorists actually treated with reverence and, at least to a degree, as heroes? They teach. They have all the money they need. They write books that are published and get reviewed in the *New York Times*. They launch political careers. In other words, they prosper from their crimes rather than pay for them.

That's the real lesson of the William Ayers and Bernardine Dohrn story. Barack Obama is simply a sideshow. But their support for him is worth noting. The fact that he isn't required to answer for that relationship is an illustration of how much violent, left-wing, infantile, socialist anti-Americanism is accepted within the Democratic Party, academia, the establishment news media, and other key cultural institutions.

Of course, Barack Obama can't understand why his relationship with these people would be offensive to normal, rational, thinking, and well-informed Americans with a conscience. He is, after all, a product of these same cultural institutions. He is the native son of the new covertly subversive Democratic Party.

That brings us to a more well-known scandal engulfing Barack Obama—one that very nearly did him in politically in the primaries and one from which he was never able to recapture his winning momentum against Hillary Clinton.

I refer, of course, to his pastor of twenty years—Rev. Jeremiah Wright.

Barack Obama would like us to forget about Trinity United Church of Christ and Rev. Jeremiah Wright, his spiritual guru, who provided him with the title of his campaign book, *The Audacity of Hope*.[21]

With good reason.

Wright is not only an embarrassment now to Obama; he's an embarrassment to the entire country.

Yet, it would be wrong to forget about Wright—to stop probing into what he said and the influence he had on his spiritual disciple.

Until earlier this year, Obama was happy to explain to anyone who would listen the powerful part Wright and the church played in his life, in shaping his worldview, in filling a spiritual void in his life, in providing the missing foundation for his own values.

In fact, that's just what Obama did back in 2006 in a speech that should be read by everyone who thinks it's time to "move on" from the Jeremiah Wright matter.

It was in Wright's church that Obama experienced what he describes as a dramatic spiritual conversion that reshaped his life and gave it new meaning.

"I was working with churches, and the Christians who I worked with recognized themselves in me," he said. "They saw that I knew their Book and that I shared their values and sang their songs. But they sensed that a part of me remained removed, detached, that I was an observer in their midst."[22]

Notice that Obama was working with many churches as a community organizer. That means he was undoubtedly exposed to all kinds of teachings, all kinds of theological viewpoints, all kinds of political and spiritual perspectives. Yet, he made a choice—to join Jeremiah Wright's church, walk down that particular aisle, get married in that particular sanctuary, get his children baptized by that particular pastor, and support that particular congregation with his significant tithes and offerings.

Why?

"For one thing, I believed and still believe in the power of the African American religious tradition to spur social change, a power made real by some of the leaders here today," he said. "Because of its past, the black church understands in an intimate way the biblical call to feed the hungry and clothe the naked and challenge powers and principalities. And in its historical struggles for freedom and the rights of man, I was able to see faith as more than just a comfort to the weary or a hedge against death, but rather as an active, palpable agent in the world. As a source of hope."[23]

Well, that would explain why he chose to join the black church, but why Jeremiah Wright's particular church?

"It was because of these newfound understandings that I was finally able to walk down the aisle of Trinity United Church of Christ on 95th Street in the South Side of Chicago one day and affirm my Christian faith," Obama said. "It came about as a choice, and not an epiphany. I didn't fall out in church. The questions I had didn't magically disappear. But kneeling beneath that cross on the South Side, I felt that I heard God's spirit beckoning me. I submitted myself to His will and dedicated myself to discovering His truth."[24]

Obama recognizes that was a significant decision, one that shaped the way he sees the world and responds to it.

"That's a path that has been shared by millions upon millions of Americans—evangelicals, Catholics, Protestants, Jews, and Muslims alike; some since birth, others at certain turning points in their lives," he said. "It is not something they set apart from the rest of their beliefs and values. In fact, it is often what drives their beliefs and their values."[25]

I couldn't agree more.

Barack H. Obama's most basic beliefs and values were either shaped or affirmed in Jeremiah Wright's pulpit in the Trinity United Church of Christ. There is simply no way around that. Barack H. Obama told us so himself not that long ago.

How important is Jeremiah Wright to Barack Obama?

He's so important that, until Wright was forced to step down, he had an official leadership role in Obama's campaign for the presidency.

Yet, Obama insisted for weeks later he did not think of his retired pastor in political terms.

After listening to this America-hating, racist demagogue, it's hard for me to think of him in anything *but* political terms.

Are these homilies from his sermons spiritual, or are they political?

- "The government gives them the drugs, builds bigger prisons, passes a three strikes law and then wants us to sing 'God bless America.' No, no, no, not 'God bless America,' God damn America—that's in the Bible, you're killing innocent people, God damn America for treating us citizens as less than human."[26]

- "We bombed Hiroshima, we bombed Nagasaki and we nuked far more than the thousands in New York and the Pentagon, and we never batted an eye.... America's chickens are coming home to roost."[27]

- "We've got more black men in prison than there are in college. Racism is alive and well. Racism is how this country was founded and how this country is still run. No black man will ever be considered for president, no matter how hard you run Jesse [Jackson] and no black woman can ever be considered for anything outside what she can give with her body."[28]

- "America is still the No. 1 killer in the world.... We are deeply involved in the importing of drugs, the exporting of guns and the training of professional killers.... We bombed Cambodia, Iraq and Nicaragua, killing women and children while trying to get public opinion turned against Castro and Gadhafi.... We put [Nelson] Mandela in prison and supported *apartheid* the whole twenty-seven years he was there. We believe in white supremacy and black inferiority and believe it more than we believe in God."[29]

- "We supported Zionism shamelessly while ignoring the Palestinians and branding anybody who spoke out against it as being anti-Semitic.... We care nothing about human life if the end justifies the means...."[30]

- "We started the AIDS virus.... We are only able to maintain our level of living by making sure that Third World people live in grinding poverty."...[31]

To this, Obama actually said, with a straight face, "I don't think that my church is actually particularly controversial."[32]

Remember, Wright married Michelle and Barack Obama and baptized their children.

Finally, after weeks of public revelations of what his pastor believes and preaches, the heat finally got too great and Obama was forced to distance himself from his longtime spiritual mentor. After pledging he would never turn his back on Wright any more than he would turn his back on the black community, Obama threw Wright under the bus as a matter of political expediency.

But the political necessities of the moment aside, what does it tell us about Obama and his candidacy that for twenty years he and his wife have been following this raving lunatic? He either has no judgment, no discernment; or he tacitly agrees with the filth he has been listening to preached from the pulpit for the last two decades.

Imagine yourself sitting in church on Sunday and hearing some of the above. What would you do? Would you continue attending such a church? Would you choose it as the place to get married? Would you choose this pastor as the one to baptize your children? Would you be a member for two decades? Would you dedicate your book to him? Would you appoint him to a leadership position in your campaign?

That's what Barack Obama did, as amazing as that may seem.

There is simply no other explanation than that Obama essentially agrees with the substance of what Wright says.

I believe it's what Michelle Obama believes, too.

Michelle Obama stunned the country when she said, earlier this year, she was proud of America for the first time in her life because of her husband's electoral success.

"What we have learned over the past year is that hope is making a comeback," she said. "And let me tell you something—for the first time in my adult lifetime, I am really proud of my country. And not just because Barack has done well, but because I think people are hungry for change. And I have been desperate to see our country moving in that

34

direction and just not feeling so alone in my frustration and disappointment."[33]

Later, in a *New Yorker* profile, she was quoted in a stump speech made throughout South Carolina as characterizing America as "just downright mean."[34]

She said the country is divided, life is not good, the people are "guided by fear" and cynicism.[35]

"We have become a nation of struggling folks who are barely making it every day," she told churchgoers in that primary state. "Folks are just jammed up, and it's gotten worse over my lifetime."[36]

She went on to complain that college is too expensive, schools are not doing the job, healthcare is out of reach, and pensions are disappearing.

"Let me tell you, don't get sick in America!" she exclaimed.[37]

Does this sound like a first lady?

I also get the sense this pair would step on anyone to get to the top.

That's what hit me when I heard Barack Obama compare his white grandmother—unfavorably, I might add—to his racist hatemonger of a pastor.

In a speech hailed by his supporters as historic, Obama explained, "I can no more disown him [Rev. Jeremiah Wright] than I can disown the black community. I can no more disown him than I can my white grandmother—a woman who helped raise me, a woman who sacrificed again and again for me, a woman who loves me as much as she loves anything in this world, but a woman who once confessed her fear of black men who passed by her on the street, and who on more than one occasion has uttered racial or ethnic stereotypes that made me cringe."[38]

That was bad.

But it got worse when he tried to explain why he was telling tales out of school about what he perceives as white racism in the woman who helped raise him.

He told a radio interviewer: "She is extremely proud, and the point I was making was not that my grandmother harbors any racial animosity. She doesn't. But she is *a typical white person* who, you know, if she sees somebody on the street that she doesn't know, there is a reaction that has been bred into our experiences that don't go away and sometimes come out in the wrong way.... That's the nature of race in our society...and we have to break through it. And what makes me optimistic is you see each generation feeling a little less like that, and that's pretty powerful stuff."[39]

I have emphasized the four words that struck me in this explanation—"a typical white person."

What does that mean?

What is a typical white person?

If I said, "He's a typical black person," would such a statement not be considered racist?

It seems to me, once again, a perfect illustration of the race problem we have in this country. The politicians who spend the most time talking about racial divides are the very politicians most obsessed with race, most race-conscious, most likely to generalize and stereotype, most willing to lump people into racial and ethnic groups.

What is the definition of racism?

There are several, of course, but one definition is "prejudice based on race." Another is "discriminatory or abusive behavior toward members of another race."

I would argue that Obama's characterization of his grandmother fits both of those definitions. It reveals his belief that the "typical white person" harbors unfounded fears of black men. It also reveals his willingness to caricature even his own grandmother—abuse her, if you will—as a racist in the biggest speech of his life, one that was carefully crafted for maximum political advantage.

Do I exaggerate?

I don't think so.

If you don't support preferential treatment of blacks and other minorities based on their skin color and ancestry, just try referring to someone as a "typical black person" and see what happens.

If, however, you do support these paternalistic, plantation-mentality kinds of race preferences, it's perfectly all right to stereotype—as Barack Obama supporters did in trying to explain that Jeremiah Wright's hate speech was "typical" of what can be heard in black churches across the country.

I don't believe that. I think that kind of racist, anti-Americanism is exceptional in U.S. black churches. But it was Barack Obama who, until he finally did "disown" Jeremiah Wright, found "nothing particularly controversial" about his church.

So who are the racists?

Are they the people who believe all individuals should be treated fairly and equitably?

Or are they the people who believe some individuals, because of their race, are in need of special help?

Until I heard him trash his grandma, I thought of Barack Obama as a seriously misguided political demagogue. Then I began thinking of him as someone so ambitious for political power, he would step on his own kin if it made him look better to one potential voter.

Also, Obama has made it clear he will use race when it benefits him in his political quest, but it's not fair for anyone not supporting him to mention it.

In other words, he wants to be America's first affirmative-action president. Former Democratic Party vice presidential nominee Geraldine Ferraro's candid remarks about the way she views Obama's campaign for the presidency illustrate some of the fundamental flaws of the Democrats' fondness for dividing America into racial, sexual, and class constituencies.

Ferraro now admits she would never have been chosen as the vice presidential running mate of Walter Mondale in 1984 had she been a man.

She also asserted, as an active supporter of Hillary Clinton's candidacy, that Obama would not be where he is today if he were white. She also hinted at sexism in his campaign and within the media covering Clinton. "I think what America feels about a woman becoming president takes a very secondary place to Obama's campaign—to a kind of campaign that it would be hard for anyone to run against," she said. "For one thing, you have the press, which has been uniquely hard on her. It's been a very sexist media. Some just don't like her. The others have gotten caught up in the Obama campaign. If Obama was a white man, he would not be in this position. And if he was a woman (of any color) he would not be in this position. He happens to be very lucky to be who he is. And the country is caught up in the concept." [40]

Is what she said about Obama true?

Of course it is. What is amazing is that few others have said it—out loud. It took a prominent member of Obama's own race-conscious party and a champion of affirmative-action politics to say it.

Is what she said about Clinton true?

Of course it is not. She, too, is a beneficiary of affirmative action politics—a wholly unqualified candidate whose greatest asset is the misguided notion that it is time for a woman to be president.

It was almost amusing to watch this inartful spectacle as special-interest group politics catches up with the Democratic Party practitioners of this degrading, demeaning, and exploitive ideology. Now, perhaps, even promoters of affirmative action can see how the policy hurts the very people it is supposedly intended to help.

Even well-qualified blacks and women who get coveted jobs and positions will always be suspected, by at least a certain percentage of the public, of having been the beneficiaries of racial or sexual preference policies. That is not good for blacks or women. And it's not good for a society based on equality under the law.

It seems the chickens are coming home to roost within the Democratic Party, which practically invented this insidious form of socially acceptable racism and sexism.

All kinds of admissions are being made as feminists are pitted against black liberals. It took Ferraro twenty-four years to acknowledge what the rest of America has known all that time—that she was the vice presidential nominee of her party only because she was a prominent woman.

Obama has another not-so-endearing quality as a politician. He makes things up. And almost all the stuff he makes up is unflattering to America.

For instance, if you listen to Barack Obama, you might get the impression Arab American families are getting knocks on their doors in the middle of the night, after which they are spirited away to concentration camps, never to be seen again.

As the head of an Arab American family, this was news to me.

But that's what he told the members of his party when he gave the keynote address at the 2004 Democratic National Convention.

"If there is an Arab American family being rounded up without benefit of an attorney, it threatens my civil liberties," he said. "It is that fundamental belief, I am my brother's keeper, I am my sister's keeper, it is that fundamental belief that makes this country work."[41]

Granted, he said "if." But that is an awfully big "if." I don't think there will be much emphasis on the word "if" when that message is played on Al Jazeera and around the Muslim world, where it is assumed America routinely rounds up innocent Arab Americans without trial, without attorneys, without reason.

Does Barack Obama actually believe Arab American families are being rounded up? Does he believe any have been rounded up? Does he believe it will happen?

Does his contempt for American institutions know no depths?

Is this one of the reasons he and his wife have had no pride in their country until he became a front-running presidential candidate?

Can he name one Arab American family that has ever been mistreated by the U.S. government?

Why is he singling out Arab American families? Does he think they deserve special consideration?

Is he afraid his family might be rounded up because of his own Arab African name?

Is this one of the reasons he seems to so rarely make public reference to his middle name, Hussein—which is clearly Arab in origin?

Let me tell you, as an Arab American, I believe my chances for being a victim of any mass roundup will be greatly increased through a Barack Hussein Obama presidency. It won't come because of my ethnic background. But, if it does come, it will likely be because of my open allegiance to constitutional government—something this self-proclaimed "constitutional scholar" wouldn't understand if the document read itself to him.

Think of the damage this man does to his nation's image around the world every time he opens his mouth. It's disgraceful. It's treacherous. It's pathological.

But there's more to the quote, if you remember. Barack Obama is noted for speaking in platitudes and non sequiturs—and this is no exception.

He jumps in his speech before the Democratic National Convention from portraying America as a police state to explaining that it is America's charitable instincts and its commitment to compassion for others that make it work.

Which is it?

Or is it really both?

Is he concerned about the oppressive power of the state? Or does he actually plan to make the oppressive state more powerful—to grow it at the expense of individual compassion, which he finds lacking in its inability to solve any real problems?

Think about these questions and this quote, because they say a lot about the man most likely to be the next president of the United States.

As an Arab American, I am deeply offended that this man claims to be protecting my rights, watching out for my family's welfare, serving as my loving brother.

He's not. My Arab American family has been in this country for three generations, having fled the persecution of the Muslim world in search of a better life. Never once has any member of my extended family, going back three generations, experienced even the slightest discrimination or bigotry in this wonderful land of opportunity and promise. Certainly we have never quaked in our beds fearing a knock on the door or an extra-judicial roundup.

It is so preposterous. It is so demeaning. It is so insulting to America.

I'm sure America's enemies are putting Barack Obama's campaign rhetoric to use in their propaganda at this very moment. What a field day they will have if he is elected!

Obama, by the way, claims to be a committed Christian. As a committed Christian myself, I find that difficult to believe based on his positions. Let's examine, for instance, his position on abortion.

Here's a guy who is usually so confident, so well-spoken, so self-assured, so articulate.

Usually.

But if you want to see him whither and melt, grow uneasy, be at a loss for words, become tentative, halting, just ask him one of the simplest and most profound questions to be debated in the public square in the last thirty-five years—since he was twelve years old.

The question: "Do you believe life begins at conception, and if not, when does it begin?"

He stuttered. He stammered. He squirmed. He reached for words that failed him. He finally admitted he hadn't really come to grips with one of the hottest public policy issues of our time.

"This is something I have not come to a firm resolution on," he finally managed.[42]

Now try to imagine this man going toe-to-toe with Mahmoud Ahmadinejad or Kim Jong-il or Hu Jintao or Vladimir Putin.

The man cannot even express coherently what he believes about when human life begins.

And despite the gibberish coming out of his mouth, he *has* studied this issue. He has been coached on it. He knows what he believes. He has voted on this issue as a state legislator in Illinois and as a U.S. senator in Washington.

He has staked out an extreme position in favor of abortion on demand—even when it comes to late-term, partial-birth abortions, unnecessary for any medical purpose, that involve the cold-blooded execution of fully developed preborn babies by plunging scissors into their skulls without the courtesy of anesthesia.[43]

I doubt such a procedure would be legal for dogs in America. I doubt very much Barack Obama would attempt to justify such a horrific procedure by veterinarians. Yet he opposed the ban on partial-birth abortion, which even many of his fellow Democrats recognize is no different than infanticide.

He also was not short of words when he denounced the U.S. Supreme Court's decision upholding the partial-birth ban.

He had no trouble mustering the decisiveness to oppose a bill in the Illinois Senate that would have simply prevented the subsequent killing outside the womb of infants who survived abortion procedures. By his actions, Obama said the lives of these babies who survived the violence of abortion were just mistakes that needed to be erased by any means necessary.

And, if his record on when life begins wasn't clear enough from his actions as a legislator, recall how he didn't want his own daughters "punished with a baby."[44]

Those statements and actions by Barack Obama about his position on when life begins are far more articulate than his babbling at the Pennsylvania candidate forum.

There's no doubt about where this monster stands on this hideous procedure—any more than there is doubt about where Hillary Clinton stands.

Their policies can apparently be summarized as follows: When in doubt, abort. In most cases, babies are like a kind of parasitic disease. They need to be surgically removed like a cancer. Even moments before they are ready to be born, abortionists should be allowed to exterminate them with extreme prejudice. And if, by some miracle, these helpless babes should survive that pain and injury, then they should be finished off outside the womb.

That is the position of Barack Obama. If he is elected president, it will be open season on unborn babies. But, of course, it already is open season. It has been since 1973.

There's more to the case against Barack Obama—sadly, much more.

If America is not careful, it could soon see one-seventh of its gross domestic product nationalized—the biggest step toward socialism this country has ever taken.

That's what will happen if Barack Obama is elected president and the Democrats control the Congress.

The consequences of placing the nation's healthcare system under the control of the federal government cannot be overstated. It will be a disaster on several fronts:

- Another stake in the heart of the world's oldest constitution, which strictly limits the powers of Congress and nowhere suggests it has any authority over matters of healthcare and medicine in what has been the freest country on the face of the earth.

- Contrary to popular opinion, "free" healthcare is actually the most expensive kind—paid for with massively higher taxes and regulations that drive up medical costs exponentially.

- It will costs lives, as healthcare is rationed for the first time in America and patients are forced to wait for or forgo medical services they would like to have.

None of these observations is new, of course. They have all been made by others—many times. Yet Americans seem hell-bent on turning over control of their own healthcare destiny to lawyers and politicians in Washington.

It's mystifying.

One of the ways demagogues like Hillary Clinton and Barack Obama have convinced Americans of the need to enslave themselves to government healthcare nannies is by linking insurance (private or taxpayer-supported) to medical access

They suggest there are 47 million Americans without healthcare because there are 47 million without some form of insurance. It's just not true. Hospitals in America don't turn away indigent patients. In fact, it's against the law.

So, it's accurate to say there are no Americans—even illegal aliens!—who are without basic medical care.

Another argument they use is that healthcare costs are going up so rapidly that even more people will be denied insurance and medical care in the future. In this case, the argument is not entirely specious; however, it is more of a self-fulfilling prophecy, as anyone who understands Economics 101 can explain.

The primary reason healthcare costs are exploding in the United States is because fewer people are actually paying for healthcare themselves. As insurance and government programs like Medicare take on greater proportions of the costs, the costs go up. There is far less accountability when third parties are paying the bills.

Let me give you an example of how this works: There are some kinds of medical care that are more affordable today than ever before. One example is LASIK surgery. The price of these treatments for the eyes is not going up; it's coming down. Do you know why? Principally, because insurance doesn't cover the procedure—and neither does Medicare. Isn't that amazing? When people themselves have to bear the costs of treatments, the price doesn't go up; it actually comes down!

What's missing from the political debate about healthcare are ideas about how to bring down the cost—to make it more affordable. The answer is *not* nationalizing the industry. The answer is *not* doing more of the same. The answer is *not* 100 percent third-party payments. The answer is *not* less accountability to the patients.

But that's what Obama and most of the Democrats in Congress believe is the answer.

Too many Americans agree with them—because they are just not smart enough to see through the smokescreen.

This is not a plan for better healthcare. It's a plan for a power grab by government. When the smoke clears, you won't have your money or the healthcare you were promised.

I know there's little chance anyone will listen to this plea. After all, it is so far removed from what passes as conventional wisdom today. There is a problem in the healthcare industry. Medical care is getting too expensive. The answer is to take steps that will reduce the cost—not make it more palatable for the industry to charge even higher rates because no one cares about the bills anymore.

It's tough to fight the tide. But the answer is disengaging government encroachment into healthcare, rather than having government take over the industry.

Remember where you heard this. Someday you or someone you love will be seeking permission of a government bureaucrat to have a lifesaving procedure. Someday you or someone you love will be told you have to wait for that surgery. Someday you or someone you love may be told you're just not a good candidate for that treatment.

It's inevitable. This cockamamie social experiment has been tried again and again. The results are always the same. There's nothing new under the sun. There is no free lunch. And there is no such thing as free medical care.

And it's just further evidence of what has been a drift toward socialism in America. If Barack Obama is elected, that drift will become a runaway train.

The famous American socialist Norman Thomas has often been quoted as saying, "The American people will never knowingly adopt socialism, but under the name of liberalism they will adopt every fragment of the socialist program until one day America will be a socialist nation without ever knowing how it happened."

I've been thinking deeply about those famously prophetic words spoken by America's premier socialist thinker and leader.

They didn't resonate in the 1930s when Franklin Roosevelt, in the name of ending the Depression, exceeded all constitutional authority by approving new federal assistance programs.

They seemed a bit far-fetched to most of us in the 1960s when Lyndon Johnson vastly expanded the welfare state in his failed bid to end poverty in America.

They still didn't connect in the 1970s when Richard Nixon, in a bid to ingratiate himself with Democrats in Congress and stave off an impeachment, greatly increased spending on wealth redistribution schemes.

And by the 1980s, with Ronald Reagan in power, it seemed this forty-year trend had finally been reversed.

But with the initiatives being proposed by Barack Obama in the 2008 presidential campaign, it appears Norman Thomas was right all along. Americans will, indeed, embrace every fragment of the socialist program in the name of liberalism.

Perhaps the most startling of all is his proposal known as the Global Poverty Act. It would, in the next decade, transfer at least $845 billion of U.S. taxpayer money overseas. Think of Johnson's failed war on poverty going international—directed not by Americans but by the United Nations. How we could even be debating ideas like this in the twenty-first century, after all of the climactic failures of socialism around the world, is amazing to me. But we're not really debating them. It seems we're not even capable as a people of debating them, reasoning over them, using our brains to consider them.

Americans may simply be too far gone spiritually, morally, and intellectually to reject the temptations of socialism.

Socialism is antithetical to human nature, yet it has great appeal to the human mind.

It's one of the great lies of all time—similar to the one told by the deceiver in the Garden of Eden. You can be like God! You can have it all right here on Earth. You can live in utopia, and you don't have to obey the laws of the universe to achieve it.

That's the essence of socialism. And it is finally seducing America, as it has seduced much of the rest of the world over the last century.

Socialism won't end poverty—in America or anywhere else. Socialism will *increase* poverty, as it has every time it has been tried in history.

Little is known about Barack Obama's actual record as a legislator. That's because he so quickly emerged on the national scene—and because most of my colleagues in the press are enamored of him.

I've studied his record—and it is not pretty. But I was struck by his response to a question he got in the Cleveland primary campaign debate when he was asked which Senate vote he would take back if he could.

Now, keep in mind, in his four years as a freshman senator from Illinois, Obama has already cast hundreds of votes. He has also *failed* to cast dozens and dozens of votes on some of the most important and controversial legislation debated in the upper house as he campaigned across the country in his bid for the presidency. (He has missed 40 percent of the Senate votes in the current session.)

But let's examine some of Obama's key votes:

- On May 24, 2007, he voted against continued funding of our troops in Iraq. He was one of only fourteen negative votes, meaning most of his Democratic colleagues opposed him.

- On January 11, 2007, he voted against reform of earmarks, the basis of pork-barrel spending—again contradicting the majority of his fellow Democrats.

- On June 22, 2006, he voted against procurement of F-22A fighter aircraft and F-119 engines—again contradicting the majority of his fellow Democrats.

- On May 17, 2006, he voted against an increase in the amount of fencing and vehicle barriers along the southwest border of the United States—again contradicting the majority of his fellow Democrats.

- On September 29, 2005, he opposed the confirmation of Supreme Court Justice John Roberts.

- On August 3, 2007, he voted against expanding the power of U.S. intelligence agencies to eavesdrop on foreign terror suspects.

- On April 26, 2007, he voted to set dates for withdrawal of U.S. troops from Iraq.

- On March 29, 2007, he voted to start withdrawing troops from Iraq that coming summer.

- On July 18, 2006, he voted to allow federal funding for experimentation on embryonic stem cells.

- On June 6, 2006, he opposed a cloture motion on a same-sex marriage amendment that effectively killed it.

- On May 25, 2006, he voted for a "comprehensive immigration reform" bill that would have provided amnesty to millions of illegal aliens.

- On May 11, 2006, he voted against extending President Bush's tax cuts.

- On January 31, 2006, he opposed the confirmation of Supreme Court Justice Samuel Alito.

I could go on and on. He has cast dozens and dozens of votes to spend taxpayer money on extra-constitutional programs. The *National Journal* characterized him as the most liberal senator in 2007. He's been out there—on the fringe—casting tough votes, controversial votes, extreme votes.

And that's why I thought his answer to that question at the Cleveland debate was so amazing, so unbelievable, so shocking.

What is the single, solitary, lone vote Barack Obama regrets having cast in his years in the Senate? Here's what he said:

> When I first arrived in the Senate that first year, we had a situation surrounding Terri Schiavo. And I remember how we adjourned with a unanimous agreement that eventually allowed

Congress to interject itself into that decision-making process of the families. It wasn't something I was comfortable with, but it was not something that I stood on the floor and stopped. And I think that was a mistake, and I think the American people understood that that was a mistake. And as a constitutional law professor, I knew better.... And I think that's an example of inaction, and sometimes that can be as costly as action.[45]

That "situation" surrounding Terri Schiavo was, I like to think, an earnest effort by a group of lawmakers to save the life of an innocent woman who was eventually put to death by court order—starved and dehydrated against the wishes of her mother, father, and siblings, who wished to care for her at their own expense.

That is Barack Obama's deepest legislative regret—his biggest mistake. He tried to save the life of a poor, handicapped woman who was being victimized in the most inhuman way by her estranged husband and a rogue local court.

There are plenty of other insights into Obama's character. How about his close financial and personal relationship with the convicted Tony Rezko?[46] Or what about his pledge to accept campaign spending limits, which he subsequently abandoned when he realized he could outraise his opponents? Or what about his speeches, which have lots of clichés and little substance?

Can we do better than this equivocating, immoral cliché of a man? Yes, we can!

This should give you some insight into the character of Barack Obama. It should give you a glimpse of his dark soul. It should give you a look into his hardened, politically correct heart. It should give you a picture of what this country has in store for it if he is elected president later this year.

CHAPTER THREE

THE PROBLEM WITH THE DEMOCRATIC PARTY

E VER SINCE RONALD REAGAN retired from political life, I've been voting primarily defensively in presidential elections. Since then, it hasn't been about electing Republicans to the White House. It has been about preventing Democrats from winning.

What's wrong with Democrats? Why are their party leaders so bad, across the board, that voting against them has become, for many, the central political motivation of our time?

This will be tough for some of you to hear. It's not "politically correct." But it is the harsh truth and someone needs to say it: the national Democratic Party is immoral to the core. Any American who would vote for Democrats is guilty of fostering the worst kind of degeneracy. The leaders of this party are severely out of touch with mainstream, traditional American values. They are crusaders for perversion, for licentiousness, for nihilism, and for worse.

There, I've said it. Now let me defend it.

I've always been straight with my readers. I am not a political partisan. I find little in the Republican Party to please me. I am on record as stating I did not vote for George W. Bush in 2000 and regret voting for him defensively (against

John Kerry) in 2004. So, I think I bring more than a little objectivity to this issue.

I could write about the party's stands on various issues of the day—from unrestricted abortion on demand to the war in Iraq. But let's put this in more specific terms. Let's not talk about the macro side of the equation. Let's bring it down to the micro observations.

One day, about five years ago, I visited the Web site of the Democratic National Committee (DNC). And what did I find?

Under upcoming events I found one listing. What do you suppose it was for? Do you think it was for the Iowa Caucuses? Do you think it might have been for a political fund-raiser? Nope.

It was promoting a reception by the Gay and Lesbian Leadership Council of the DNC with the cast members of *Queer Eye for the Straight Guy*. It seems the council, which I suspect wields a powerful role in the party, had set up the "Bloody Mary Brunch" in New York as it continued its "quest to make over the White House in 2004."

Again, this was not one of twenty upcoming events sponsored by the DNC. It was not one of ten. It was the *only* event listed on the national organization's Web site.

Let's face it, this is what the Democrats were all about in 2003. And, frankly, the situation has only worsened in 2008.

Take a look at the Web site yourself today. Look at the DNC's official links. You can tell much about an organization by the Web site links—and with the DNC you're just a click away from virtually every bizarre extremist organization in America, from the American Civil Liberties Union to Planned Parenthood, to the racist National Council of La Raza, to more than a half-dozen "gay and lesbian organizations."

Birds of a feather flock together.

There is something almost frightening about the extremist nature of the Democratic Party's highest leadership. Just try to find one thing positive about American life on this Web site. It's not there. The DNC would have you believe that since the election of George W. Bush as president, America has become some kind of a fascist police state, an economic disaster area, and an oppressive, deceitful, imperialist beast around the world.

This is not what I would characterize as loyal opposition— and I'm hardly pro-Republican or pro-Bush.

These are not the Democrats your parents knew. These are not even the Democrats of George McGovern. And these are certainly not the Democrats of John F. Kennedy.

Forty-six years ago, President John F. Kennedy announced a startling economic policy change. He tried to educate the American people about why he was cutting taxes—not that the American people or any other people have ever needed to be persuaded to cut taxes.

In a news conference November 20, 1962, he said, "It is a paradoxical truth that tax rates are too high and tax revenues are too low and the soundest way to raise the revenues in the long run is to cut the rates now.... Cutting taxes now is not to incur a budget deficit, but to achieve the more prosperous, expanding economy which can bring a budget surplus."[1]

Still, twenty years later, many were skeptical when Ronald Reagan explained the same principle again. Nevertheless, the policies worked both times—to perfection.

As for Kennedy, still an icon of the modern American Democratic Party, it was not the first nor the last time he would make this point.

In his budget message to Congress on January 17, 1963, he explained, "[L]ower rates of taxation...will stimulate economic activity and so raise the levels of personal and corporate income as to yield within a few years an increased—not a reduced—flow of revenues to the federal government."[2]

He underscored the point a few days later, on January 21, 1963, in his annual address to the Congress: "In today's economy, fiscal prudence and responsibility call for tax reduction even if it temporarily enlarges the federal deficit—why reducing taxes is the best way open to us to increase revenues."[3]

Just a couple months before he was assassinated in the streets of Dallas, he made a television address to the nation on his tax-reduction bill. He told his fellow Americans on September 18, 1963: "A tax cut means higher family income and higher business profits and a balanced federal budget. Every taxpayer and his family will have more money left over after taxes for a new car, a new home, new conveniences, education and investment. Every businessman can keep a higher percentage of his profits in his cash register or put it to work expanding or improving his business, and as the national income grows, the federal government will ultimately end up with more revenues."[4]

Throughout his young life, and particularly his short presidency, Kennedy made the point over and over again— high taxes were counterproductive, a drag on the economy, hurting the very people they would supposedly help through government programs.

In spite of Kennedy's leadership on this issue—and despite the historic evidence we have to show his policies worked— those who continue to idolize him today, members of his party, even members of his family, don't seem to get it. Or, if they do, they ignore the evidence for their own selfish reasons.

But you can't change history. You can ignore it at your own peril. You can attempt to distort it for your own benefit. You can purposely hide uncomfortable facts. However, John F. Kennedy said these things and he followed through with actions. There is simply no denying this reality.

The Democratic Party elite of 2008 is the generation that knew not JFK. They have succumbed to an evil ideology inflicting massive suffering, misery, injustice, oppression, and death wherever it gains power and influence. This ideology proffers that it is a good idea to forcibly take the wealth and property rightfully and legally acquired by one party and redistribute it to others. Of course, Democrats and many

Republicans who think like them always take a sizable cut of the transaction for themselves—sometimes as much as 80 percent.

My friend Walter Williams accurately describes this process as "legalized theft."[5] There is no better way to explain it. Legalized theft is the central creed of the modern Democratic Party among the generation that knew not JFK. All manner of justifications and rationalizations are made for this process—the greater good, helping the poor, leveling the playing field. No matter what you call it, theft is theft.

But theft is only the beginning of the evil Democrats spread.

Democrats also kill.

They kill in a thousand different ways. Let me give you a few:

- According to the National Right to Life Committee, since the 1973 *Roe v. Wade* Supreme Court ruling, almost 50 million unborn babies have been killed in America.[6] Democrats, in general, seem to have more respect and reverence for bald eagle eggs than unborn humans.

- By actively working to disarm the American population, in direct violation of the U.S. Constitution, Democrats condemn the defenseless to death—often at the hands of criminals they help spring from prison.

- Through opposition to missile defense and civil defense, Democrats leave the entire civilian population open to annihilation at the hands of a nuclear-armed madman, an accidental launch by a nuclear power, and terrorist attacks.

- Through careless over-deployment of the armed forces all over the world and wars like

Vietnam, Democrats kill U.S. soldiers and foreign soldiers and civilians without so much as a care about the constitutional basis for their actions.

The Democratic Party leadership of the twenty-first century is viciously anti-American and is ready, willing, and able to make unfounded, undocumented, untrue, reckless charges against their country without any regard to how those assertions will be used by U.S. enemies.

This year, such statements have been flowing directly from the mouths of Barack and Michelle Obama.

In remarks about U.S. policy in Iraq, Barack Obama told an election-night gathering in San Antonio, Texas on March 4, 2008 that America was a bully: "It's the same course that continues to divide and isolate America from the world by substituting bluster and bullying for direct diplomacy."[7]

Michelle Obama, as I mentioned in the previous chapter, angered many Americans when she said her husband's ascendancy politically coincided with her being proud of her country "for the first time in her adult life" and characterized the United States in campaign stops as "downright mean."

To me, an Arab American, the most offensive comment made by Barack Obama lately is actually one he has been using in speeches since 2004 (he first said it at the Democratic National Convention that year): "If there is an Arab American family being rounded up without benefit of an attorney, it threatens my civil liberties."[8]

Before I go on, let me first answer these outlandish and irresponsible statements.

America is not a bully. If Obama thinks America is acting as a bully somewhere in the world, he should be very specific about that instance, rather than hurl this kind of broad invective, which serves only our enemies' propaganda machines.

America is not "downright mean." Anyone who believes that and states it openly should be instantly disqualified from high office by voters. America is the most compassionate country on earth. Saying otherwise only plays into the hands of those who seek to destroy us.

America is not, never has, and never will round up Arab American families without benefit of an attorney. Barack Obama knows this. But he chooses to lie about his country, giving credence to the most anti-American myths being perpetuated by radical Islamists and other U.S. haters around the world.

If this kind of America-bashing were limited to the Obama family, it would still be shameful, given his status as the Democratic nominee for the presidency—the head of his party. Unfortunately, these spiteful, treacherous, anti-American insults have become common verbal currency for Democratic Party leaders.

Let's go back to February 2006. Former Vice President Al Gore, the choice of his party to be president in 2000, speaking in Saudi Arabia, told his foreign audience that Arabs in the United States had been "indiscriminately rounded up, often on minor charges of overstaying a visa or not having a green card in proper order, and held in conditions that were just unforgivable. Unfortunately, there have been terrible abuses and it's wrong. I do want you to know that it does not represent the desires or wishes or feelings of the majority of the citizens of my country."[9]

It was all a lie. There had been no such roundups. But it played well in Saudi Arabia and throughout the Arab Muslim world—at that very moment inflamed to the point of murder over some Muhammad cartoons.

In 2007, former president Bill Clinton was on foreign soil, proclaiming his role in his wife's future administration would be as a kind of roving ambassador whose job would be to "go out and immediately restore America's standing, go out and tell people America was open for business and cooperation again" after eight years marked by unilateralist policies that have "enrage[d] the world."[10] How about another former Democratic president—Jimmy Carter? In 2005, also on foreign soil, Carter called the war in Iraq "unnecessary and unjust" and said the treatment of prisoners at Guantanamo Bay provided "impetus and excuses to potential terrorists to lash out at our country and justify their despicable acts."[11] In fact, Carter virtually campaigned for the Nobel Peace Prize by attacking America. And when he won the award, the committee specifically cited this and said they hoped to send a message to Bush.[12]

Ronald Reagan's U.N. ambassador, Jeanne Kirkpatrick, famously characterized the Democrats back in 1984 as the "blame-America-first" party. It was accurate then and it is accurate today.

But it seems to me the rhetoric is growing more abusive toward our country. The Democrats have morphed from the "blame-America-first" party to the "I-hate-America" party.

One of the ways the Democrats portray America as evil is to make up, out of whole cloth, statistics and horror stories about the way children are oppressed and victimized in the country. Democrats love to portray themselves as the advocates for children.

For instance, when Barack Obama was asked by the late Tim Russert whether he believed there was life on other planets, the candidate said: "You know, I don't know, and I don't presume to know. What I know is there is life here on Earth and that we're not attending to life here on Earth. We're not taking care of kids who are alive and, unfortunately, are not getting healthcare. We're not taking care of senior citizens who are alive and are seeing their heating prices go up."[13]

Yet, if I had Barack Obama's glass-house record on children and old folks, I'm not sure I would be throwing stones like that.

What do I mean?

Well, for all their blustery talk about what they are going to do for kids and the elderly, the fact of the matter is, with Democrats in power, the most dangerous place in America is in the mother's womb.

Obama and the Democratic Party machine will gladly tell you all the wonderful things they're going to do for children—with your money. But the truth is they won't even protect their lives, as the Constitution of the United States demands.

No examination of the Democratic Party and its immorality, indecency, and evil nature would be complete, of course, without a mention of abortion.

Marking the thirty-third anniversary of the *Roe v. Wade* Supreme Court decision striking down virtually all state laws restricting abortion, Democratic National Committee Chairman Howard Dean said the ruling "served to ensure the personal freedoms and rights of women all over the country to make decisions about their own healthcare and reproductive rights."

"As a physician and former Planned Parenthood board member, I understand that the decision to have an abortion is one of the most difficult a woman can make," he continued. "We can all agree that abortion should be rare, but it should also be safe and legal. This difficult personal healthcare decision should be made by a woman, in consultation with her physician, and not by politicians in Washington."

He concluded: "Democratic leaders are working hard to improve women's access to healthcare, and increase economic opportunities which will help to decrease the number of unintended pregnancies. And Democrats will remain steadfast in protecting the individual rights and freedoms of not only women but all Americans."[14]

I think it's safe to say that Dean's comments reflect the thinking of most of his party's politicians.

So, let's examine his statements.

Notice he doesn't reference the one critical document the U.S. Supreme Court is supposed to consider in making a ruling—the Constitution. Instead, he talks about "personal freedoms" and "the rights of women" to make decisions "about their own healthcare and reproductive rights."

From where does this "personal freedom" to extinguish the life of an unborn baby come?

From where do these "rights" descend?

Do they come from the Supreme Court? Do they come from God? Are they unalienable rights like those referenced by the founders? Is the taking of the life of an unborn baby when the mother's life is not endangered really a matter of healthcare? Or is it a matter of selfish convenience and utilitarian ethics?

And then there's the subject of "reproductive rights." Do you know which countries and societies have violated the rights of parents to make decisions about reproduction and child-bearing? They are the countries and societies that emphasize abortion—countries like China that dictate to parents how many children they will be permitted to have.

Therefore, one could easily make the argument that government-approved, government-financed, and government-subsidized abortion represents the gravest threat in the history of mankind to this notion of "reproductive rights."

Dean notes for the record that he is a former board member of Planned Parenthood. That should surprise no one. Planned Parenthood is in the abortion business—big time. According to its own annual report, available on the Planned Parenthood Web site, the organization conducted almost 290,000 abortions in the 2006-2007 fiscal year alone. At the same time, the organization's own records show it has provided only 2410 adoption referrals.

Planned Parenthood is not about offering women choices. It is not about planning parenthood. It is about snuffing out the lives of as many unborn babies as it possibly can. Indeed, Planned Parenthood was founded by Margaret Sanger, who believed in the use of eugenics, which often meant babies of color were aborted.

But it is always surprising to me to hear an abortion proponent like Dean tell us: "I understand that the decision to have an abortion is one of the most difficult a woman can make. We can all agree that abortion should be rare, but it should also be safe and legal."

Why should it be so? Why is the decision to have an abortion so difficult? Why should it be rare?

The answer is simple: because it is killing. It represents the taking of an innocent life by someone else. Dean knows that. Planned Parenthood knows that. Deep down in our souls, all of us know that.

And that's why it is perfectly appropriate and moral to have laws restricting the practice. That's precisely what our Constitution requires our federal government to do—to protect the lives and property of its citizens and their "posterity." One definition of "posterity" is those yet to be born.

The Constitution is very specific about abortion. You don't need to read between the lines. You don't need to read the minds of the founders. You can just read the simple, plain, English-language words they used in the preamble to the Constitution to see what they clearly meant.

The only way we can justify this practice as a "right" is to resort to Orwellian redefinition of the simplest, clearest terms. And that's what Dean, most members of his party, and too many members of the other party do to excuse abortion, to rationalize it—even, arguably, to *glorify* it.

Dean also says, "This difficult personal healthcare decision should be made by a woman, in consultation with her physician, and not by politicians in Washington." On both ends of the age spectrum, Democrats are, to say the least, squishy about the right to life.

They believe an unborn child's life can be taken for any reason or no reason at all right up until the day of birth. They also believe the elderly and the infirm can be euthanized like dogs without their consent.

And we're supposed to trust *them* to help children and old folks?

Come on!

If they take complete power in 2008, as they plan, your federal tax dollars will be subsidizing abortion deaths and the involuntary deaths of handicapped people and senior citizens. I guarantee it.

That's where they are taking us. That is their agenda. It should be clear for all to see.

Yet, plenty of Americans are being fooled. They really think they have a "right" to health insurance. No one has a right to health insurance. We have a right to work hard so we can buy the things we want in life. But no one has a right to health insurance any more than we have a right to food. No one has a right to a house, either. It's up to each of us to exercise responsibility, work hard, and set priorities about what is important to each of us.

At this point, Obama and the Democrats would say: "Well, what about children? They don't have the ability to work for health insurance. Don't they have a right to it?"

There isn't anyone I know who wouldn't help a child in need. There isn't any hospital in America that would deny a child in need. But creating new "rights," as the Democrats want to do, actually ensures just the opposite. It doesn't encourage compassion. It doesn't encourage responsibility by parents. It shuffles the responsibility to "government" — to you, the taxpayer.

And, remember, if government bestows a "right" on you, it can just as easily take it away.

After all the incentives toward personal responsibility are broken down, after government has taken over healthcare and other essential programs formerly within the purview of family, government will be in a position to start determining who will live and who will die.

This is so simple, yet many Americans are about to be seduced into taking a bite out of this apple.

Question: Do you know why so many Americans are ready to give up a little bit more of their freedom and see a little bit less of their paycheck every week for a nationalized healthcare program?

Answer: Because most Americans have not yet experienced the horrors of socialized medicine firsthand.

That's why.

That's the only reason.

But, in this global village we keep hearing about, it is getting more difficult to hide the shortcomings of what will soon become known in this country as ObamaCare.

In England, for instance, it is not at all unusual for patients to be denied needed surgery because they refuse or are unable to quit smoking.

Earlier this year, we heard about the case of former builder John Nuttall, fifty-seven, who broke his ankle in three places. He has endured constant pain since, because doctors refuse to surgically rebuild the ankle because Nuttall can't or won't quit smoking.

Instead, doctors affiliated with the national health program prescribe him daily doses of morphine.

"I have begged them to operate but they won't," says Nuttall. "I have tried my hardest to give up smoking but I can't. I want to warn other smokers. We have paid our national insurance stamps all our lives and now we are being shut out."[15]

It's cruel. It's barbaric. It's ridiculous beyond words. And it is exactly what will happen here someday if we don't wise up and recognize we are giving away our freedom every time we accept another government program to "make our lives better."

How would you like to be Mr. Nuttall?

How would you like to live in a country where you are denied needed medical care because of bureaucratic red tape or shortages or rationing?

You might ask, What does smoking have to do with a broken ankle?

Doctors make the case that smoking has a very big influence on the outcome of this kind of foot surgery and that the healing process might be hindered significantly in a smoker.

So what?

Does that mean the patient must suffer in torment? What are the healing chances if surgery is not performed?

Get ready for this in the United States beginning in 2009 if a Democratic Congress and President Barack Obama believe you voted for nationalized healthcare in the next election.

What's it going to be for you?

Do you want to live in a nanny-state where decisions about your welfare and your lifestyle are made by government bureaucrats?

Or do you want to preserve what's left of freedom in this country—maybe even expand it, as our brave ancestors did?

Time is running out.

Right now, political inertia is pushing us closer and closer to nationalized, socialized medicine in this country. It's not just Democrats supporting it anymore; Republicans are tripping over themselves to show how compassionate they are, too.

Decide now. The choice is clear—freedom or servitude.

The choice is also life or death.

The choice is also morality or perversion.

Remember the Democratic presidential debate at Dartmouth? I wish I could get every American to read the transcript of what the leading candidates—Hillary Clinton, John Edwards, and Barack Obama—all had to say about the teaching of homosexuality and same-sex marriage to *second graders!*

This was the question that triggered the responses: "The issues surrounding gay rights have been hotly debated here in New England. For example, last year some parents of second-graders in Lexington, Massachusetts, were outraged to learn their children's teacher had read a story about same-sex marriage, about a prince who marries another prince. Same-sex marriage is legal in Massachusetts but most of you oppose it. Would you be comfortable having this story read to your children as part of their school curriculum?"[16]

First up was Edwards. Here's what he had to say:

> Yes, absolutely. What I want is I want my children to understand everything about the difficulties that gay and lesbian couples are faced with every day, the discrimination that they're faced with every single day of their lives. And I suspect my two younger children, Emma Claire, who's 9, and Jack, who's 7, will reach the same conclusion that my daughter Cate, who's 25, has reached, which is she doesn't understand why her dad is not in favor of same-sex marriage. And she says her generation will be the generation that brings about the great change in America on that issue. So I don't want to make that decision on behalf of my children. I want my children to be able to make that decision on behalf of themselves, and I want them to be exposed to all the information, even in—did you say second grade? Second grade might be a little tough, but even in second grade to be exposed to all those possibilities, because I don't want to impose my view. Nobody made me God. I don't get to decide on behalf of my family or my children, as my wife Elizabeth has spoken her own mind on this issue. I don't get to impose on them what it is that I believe is right. But what I will do as president of the United States is I will lead an effort to make sure that the same benefits that are available to heterosexual couples—1,100 roughly benefits in the federal government—are available to same-sex couples; that we get rid of DOMA, the Defense of Marriage Act; that we get rid of "don't ask/don't tell," which is wrong today and was wrong when it was enacted back in the 1990s. I will be the president that leads a serious effort to deal with the discrimination that exists today.

This answer left me wondering if Edwards would consider it appropriate to make sure his kids weren't eating out of the garbage can—or would he allow them to make that decision for themselves?

But, perhaps more stunning than Edwards's moronic answer were the responses of his major opponents—Barack Obama and Hillary Clinton.

They didn't take issue with anything he said. In fact, they seemed to be in general agreement with him.

Obama said, "I feel very similar to John." He went on to say his wife has already talked to his young children about same-sex marriage.

Clinton said, "I really respect what both John and Barack said." She went on to talk in generalities about tolerance and diversity.

Notice the consensus between all three of them on this subject.

That is the consensus of the Democratic Party elite. But, I have to tell you, I don't think 5 percent of Americans believe it would be appropriate to read that kind of garbage to second graders.

But here it was being defended by all three of the leading contenders for the Democratic presidential nomination.

Look at what they were all saying. Look at what the Democratic Party believes.

In all my fifty-three years on this planet, I have never read a more idiotic, mindless, pandering, scary quote than this— certainly not from a serious candidate for president of the United States.

Let's pull it apart.

"I don't want to make that decision on behalf of my children. I want my children to be able to make that decision on behalf of themselves, and I want them to be exposed to all the information."

Here's a guy running for president of the United States. He wants to make all kinds of decisions that will impact your life, the lives of your children, your neighbors, people around the world. But he doesn't want to make decisions about the moral education of his own children? And the other two running against him agree with him!

Do you believe this?

Would nothing offend them?

If their child's teacher read stories about bestiality to the class, would that bother them? Or would they reserve moral judgment? Would they let their children decide what was right in their own eyes?

I think it should be obvious from this quote that John Edwards is not only disqualified from being president of the United States, he should be disqualified from serving on a local school board. Anyone who agrees with it, as Obama and Clinton did, are also unfit to be dogcatchers. They are not only disqualified from serving on the school board; I'm thinking maybe their children should be taken away from them. They should be disqualified from responsible parenthood.

But that's not even the end of it. Look at the rest of this trial lawyer's psychobabble: "Because I don't want to impose my view—nobody made me God—I don't get to decide on behalf of my family and my children.... I don't get to impose on them what it is that I believe is right."

If parents don't get to shape the values of their children, who does?

Evidently, John Edwards believes it is the role of the state. And that is what the Democratic Party believes. It's the official position of the party.

It's kind of funny that he says, "Nobody made me God," because God actually charges parents with the responsibility of rearing their children. In other words, God wants parents to play God with their kids. He didn't leave it to professionals. He didn't leave it to schools. He didn't leave it to kings. He didn't even leave it to priests. He left child rearing to parents—and only to parents.

I've been listening to Edwards and other Democratic Party leaders make moral pronouncements about what they believe and want to do. They'll impose on us national healthcare. They'll impose on us same-sex marriage. They'll impose on us draconian energy measures to fight "global warming."

They have no problem "playing God" with our economy, with our most basic freedoms, with our Constitution, with our way of life.

But please don't ask them to make decisions about appropriate reading material for their own seven-year-old kids.

When Democrats tell you how much they want to change America and how fast, when they tell you how bad things are in our country and why, it's always important to remember they have controlled Congress for forty-one of the last fifty-three years.

During that same time, they controlled the White House twenty-six of fifty-three years.

Yet they never seem to accomplish what they promise their constituents—the elimination of poverty and homelessness, a more humane and just society, and peace with our neighbors around the world.

Why should Americans believe anything they say? Where is the credibility? Where is the track record of success?

Perhaps on one issue, the Democrats can be trusted to live up to their word. That one issue is Iraq policy. Democrats will cause a calamity in Iraq—defeat of American allies, defeat of American objectives.

In fact, throughout the last couple years, it has become increasingly obvious that one of the Democrats' biggest fears is that the United States might actually be victorious in Iraq.

For instance, in an interview last year with the *Washington Post*, James Clyburn (D-SC)., the House Democratic whip, was asked what his party would do if Gen. David Petraeus reported, as he did last fall, the surge strategy is working very well.

"Well, that would be a real big problem for us, no question about that," said Clyburn.[17]

Clyburn was simply being honest—telling us what Nancy Pelosi and Harry Reid try to disguise, camouflage, and spin to the best of their ability.

But truth is truth, and facts are facts. You know it, and I know it. The party that now controls both houses of Congress has a vested interest in military defeat for the United States in

Iraq. There is simply no other way to say it. And that is a scary and sobering reality.

The Democratic nominee for the presidency is also deeply invested in victory for al-Qaida. Think about what I am saying.

Has this ever happened before in American history?

Well, yes, it has.

It was the case in 1972, when Democrats controlled both houses of Congress and Sen. George McGovern, the father of the modern Democratic Party, was the candidate for the White House.

Those were gloomy times—with a corrupt, megalomaniacal president fighting a war with no intention of winning, a Democrat-controlled Congress hell-bent on defeat and retreat, and a radical socialist as America's political alternative.

In other words, the parallels are striking.

Yet, the enemy we faced in Vietnam was not really a threat to follow us home. True, the enemy was part of a growing international anti-American, Communist empire, but cutting and running in Vietnam would only mean a loss of prestige for the United States and the deaths of millions of innocents in Southeast Asia.

America would recover, though it would take bold new leadership eight years later in the form of Ronald Reagan.

But defeat in Iraq—a critical battlefield in a global war with Islamo-fascism, a war that has already come home— would be far more devastating to our national security.

Quite honestly, we might never recover from such a defeat.

This enemy will follow us home. This enemy has already delivered the most devastating foreign attack on our homeland in our history.

That's why this admission from Clyburn, this confirmation of what we suspected all along about the Democrats, is so significant. The worst news Democrats could hear is that the forces of good are triumphing in Iraq.

Do the Democrats not remember what happened in Vietnam? Have they persuaded themselves they were not actually responsible for the humiliating defeat America suffered as a result of their actions? Or are they just revising history in hopes of downplaying their own culpability?

In a response to one of President Bush's speeches about Iraq, Ted Kennedy called Iraq "Bush's Vietnam." And, in doing so, he explained what he meant by that characterization.

"In Vietnam, the White House grew increasingly obsessed with victory, and increasingly divorced from the will of the people and any rational policy," he explained. "There was no military solution to that war. But we kept trying to find one anyway. In the end, 58,000 Americans died in the search for it. Echoes of that disaster are all around us today. Iraq is George Bush's Vietnam."[18]

I've often said there are many living among us who apparently exist in a parallel universe—a place called "Bizarro World," where black is white, right is left, up is down, and right is wrong. Everything is backward, inverted, twisted. Ted Kennedy is one of those people. He doesn't live in Massachusetts. He lives in Bizarro World.

Kennedy, for instance, looks at Vietnam and finds the problem there was that the president, a Democrat, his late brother's vice president, was "obsessed with victory."

I lived through the Vietnam War. I've read dozens of books about it. I know many men who fought in the war. I've even met many of the policymakers responsible for conducting the conflict.

Never before Kennedy made this statement have I ever heard anyone suggest the problem in Vietnam was a preoccupation with victory. It was just the opposite. From the outset of Lyndon Johnson's escalation of the war, the goal was never "victory." The goal was to pressure the North Vietnamese Communist aggressors to accept a negotiated political solution.

Furthermore, the very phrase "obsessed with victory" betrays the total illogic and moral bankruptcy of Kennedy and his party. What's wrong with victory? To Kennedy and the Democrats, a U.S. victory is unthinkable—the worst possible outcome of a war.

I would suggest no war is worth fighting unless the goal is total victory. That was the real problem with Vietnam and the reason it turned into a disaster—the United States did not pursue victory.

Kennedy goes on to say: "There was no military solution to that war. But we kept trying to find one anyway."

How could anyone believe such a thing? The United States had recently played a large role in defeating the combined efforts of the Nazi juggernaut and imperial Japan. Does Kennedy really believe that an even stronger United States in the 1960s could not have defeated the divided country of Vietnam? It's ludicrous to even discuss it.

Clearly, the United States fought the Vietnam War with both hands tied behind its back by politicians—especially Lyndon Johnson and later Richard Nixon, who accepted the advice of Henry Kissinger that a negotiated solution was the way to go. Johnson and Nixon never even defined what victory would mean.

And that, unfortunately, is the real resemblance between Vietnam and Iraq—the inability or unwillingness to define victory and pursue it aggressively. It's the only way wars should ever be fought. Fight to win, or don't start them.

I don't know if this is a precipice from which there is any return for the party of Obama and Kennedy and Pelosi and Reid. These are people that should be considered turncoats in the truest form of the word. These are people who seem to be secretly—and now, not so secretly—praying for, hoping for, and acting in the best interests of victory for Osama bin Laden and his cohorts, who would chop off their heads just as fast as they would chop off yours and mine.

Imagine political power meaning so much to you that you would sell out your own country—perhaps even the very lives of your children and grandchildren—to retain it, consolidate it, expand it.

That's what it is all about with the Democrats. It's not about ideology. It's not that they like al-Qaida or Islamo-fascism. But they do have enough disrespect for their nation that they would tolerate—even welcome—more death, more carnage, more crisis, more 9/11s.

Can you pull the lever for that?

What I write here may seem unnecessarily harsh. But someone has to say it. The people in power today are simply not the people they are pretending to be. Take Pelosi, for instance. Or, as Henny Youngman would say, "Take Pelosi, please!"

You've heard the expression "limousine liberal."

We have lots of them in the U.S. Congress, Hollywood, and corporate boardrooms.

But I want you to know, the woman presiding over the House of Representatives is no "limousine liberal."

The phrase doesn't begin to do justice to the hypocrisy of Nancy Pelosi.

That's why I've dubbed her a "caviar commie."

It's more accurate, and I'll prove it.

Pelosi is not only the first woman speaker, she is the wealthiest.

How much is this unassuming "grandma" worth? The Center for Responsive Politics puts her in the $55 million neighborhood.[19] Pretty nice neighborhood, huh?

Despite her protestations about those "tax cuts for the rich," she has never mentioned returning them to the federal treasury, where they rightfully belong. Go figure.

Pelosi, the winner of the 2003 César Chávez award from the United Farm Workers, hires *only* non-union workers at her $25 million Napa Valley vineyard. Maybe this explains her firm opposition to any efforts to enhance border security and the flow of illegal cheap labor into the country from Mexico, speculates *Investor's Business Daily*.[20]

According to Peter Schweizer's account in *Do As I Say (Not As I Do)*, the luxury resort and restaurants she partly owns are also strictly non-union. The exclusive country club she partly owns failed to comply with existing environmental regulations for the past eight years—including a failure to protect endangered species.[21]

Those rules are for mere mortals, not the caviar Comintern.

Maybe you're saying, "Farah, I can see why Pelosi would be called a 'limousine liberal' based on what you report, but why do you take it so far as to call her a 'caviar commie'?"

Good question. And here's the rest of the story.

Pelosi is a long-time member of the "Progressive Caucus"— or, as I call it, the Congressional Red Army Caucus.

In fact, she has even served on the executive committee of the socialist-leaning Progressive Caucus, a bloc of about sixty votes, or nearly 30 percent of the minority vote in the lower chamber. Until 1999, the Web site of the Progressive Caucus was hosted by the Democratic Socialists of America (DSA). Following an *exposé* of the link between the two organizations in *WorldNetDaily*, the Progressive Caucus established its own Web site under the auspices of Congress.[22] Another officer of the Progressive Caucus, and one of its guiding lights, is avowed socialist Rep. Bernie Sanders, the Vermont independent. The Democratic Socialists of America's chief stated goal is to work within the Democratic Party and remove the stigma attached to "socialism" in the eyes of most Americans.

"Stress our Democratic Party strategy and electoral work," explains an organizing document of the DSA. "The Democratic Party is something the public understands, and association with it takes the edge off. Stressing our Democratic Party work will establish some distance from the radical subculture and help integrate you to the milieu of the young liberals."[23]

Nevertheless, the goal of the Democratic Socialists of America has never been deeply hidden. Prior to the cleanup of its Web site in 1999, the DSA included a song list featuring

"The Internationale," the worldwide anthem of communism and socialism. Another song on the site was "Red Revolution," sung to the tune of "Red Robin." The lyrics went: "When the Red Revolution brings its solution along, along, there'll be no more lootin' when we start shootin' that Wall Street throng." Another song removed after *WorldNetDaily's* exposé was "Are You Sleeping, Bourgeoisie?" The lyrics went: "Are you sleeping? Are you sleeping? Bourgeoisie, Bourgeoisie. And when the revolution comes, We'll kill you all with knives and guns, Bourgeoisie, Bourgeoisie."[24]

In the last six years, the Progressive Caucus has been careful to moderate its image for mainstream consumption.

Now, do I exaggerate when I characterize Nancy Pelosi, not as a "limousine liberal," but as a "caviar commie"?

CHAPTER FOUR

WHY McCAIN IS UNACCEPTABLE

S O FAR, I have made the case against voting for Barack Obama for president in 2008 and exposed the institutional problems of the Democratic Party that he leads. Now it is time to look at the Republican Party alternative—John McCain.

I will delineate in this chapter the reasons I cannot support McCain and why I don't believe he is a serious political alternative, but let's begin by listening to someone who sympathizes with the Democratic Party agenda.

His name is Jonathan Chait, senior editor of the *New Republic*. Here's what he wrote in that magazine February 10, 2008:

> Even though it is in the public record, McCain's voting behavior during Bush's first term is almost never mentioned in the press anymore. Yet McCain's secret history is simply astonishing. It is no exaggeration to say that, during this crucial period, McCain was the most effective advocate of the Democratic agenda in Washington.
>
> In healthcare, McCain co-sponsored, with John Edwards and Ted Kennedy, a patients' bill of rights. He joined Chuck Schumer to sponsor one bill allowing the re-importation of prescription drugs and another permitting wider sale of generic alternatives. All these measures were fiercely contested by the healthcare industry and, consequently, by Bush and the GOP leadership. On the environment, he sponsored with John Kerry a bill raising automobile fuel-efficiency standards and another bill with Joe Lieberman imposing a cap-and-trade regime on

carbon emissions. He was also one of six Republicans to vote against drilling in the Arctic National Wildlife Refuge....

McCain voted against the 2001 and 2003 Bush tax cuts. He co-sponsored bills to close the gun-show loophole, expand AmeriCorps, and federal airport security. All these things set him against nearly the entire Republican Party.[1]

It is no wonder McCain actively courted the idea of switching parties before his run for the presidency. In 2001, McCain dined with a number of Hollywood luminaries at Arianna Huffington's house. At the dinner party, his wife bragged about writing in McCain's name for president in 2000. And McCain himself allegedly claimed he didn't vote Republican in that presidential election.[2]

He clearly belongs in the Democratic Party—even in these times when there is so little distinction between the two major parties.

No matter who becomes president this year, the White House will become a bully pulpit for the religion of global warming.

No matter who becomes president this year, the White House will support federal funding of embryonic stem cell research.

No matter who becomes president this year, the White House will be in the corner of those who want more government regulation of campaign finance, meaning more restrictions on fundamental First Amendment rights.

No matter who becomes president this year, the White House will be firmly in the corner of wildly out-of-control illegal immigration, firmly opposed to building the barriers needed to suppress it, and in favor of some form of amnesty for tens of millions of illegal aliens already here.

No matter who becomes president this year, the White House will oppose tax cuts, as McCain did in 2001 and 2003.

No matter who becomes president this year, the White House will name judges and justices more in the mold of American Civil

Liberties Union political director Ruth Bader Ginsburg (whom McCain supported) than President Bush's judicial nominees defeated by the Gang of 14 (organized by McCain).

In other words, there is simply no reason for me to support McCain.

If Barack Obama is a Big Government presidential candidate with little respect for the constitutional limits on the power of the federal government, John McCain is Barack Obama lite.

How bad is McCain?

I'm afraid the answer is: very, very bad.

For starters, McCain has been, for a very long time, dead wrong on immigration and border policy. He is still dead wrong.

In 2004, voters in his own state passed Proposition 200, requiring proof of citizenship before someone can vote or participate in state giveaway programs. Despite opposition led by McCain, the measure was approved by 56 percent of the vote, with close to 50 percent of Hispanics approving it.

He's not only out of step with Americans on this issue, he's out of step even with his own constituency in Arizona.

He has been a leader in the amnesty cause in the Senate, partnering with Ted Kennedy on the bill's language and sponsorship.

He also led opposition to building the border fence.

Do you really think McCain is going to be any better than George W. Bush on this critical national priority? Chances are he will be even worse.

To underscore McCain's continuing position promoting, condoning, and excusing illegal immigration and border insecurity, in July of this year, the Republican candidate attended the national convention of La Raza in San Diego. For anyone who believed McCain was serious when he momentarily changed course during his primary campaign and pledged to build a border fence, this development should dash any such hopes.

Why do I say this?

Because I know what La Raza is all about.

The National Council of La Raza bills itself as a "civil rights" organization. It would be more appropriate to say it disguises itself as such. It camouflages itself as such. It hides its real purpose and true intents as such—with the willing and skillful assistance of many of my media colleagues.

In reality, La Raza, from many perspectives, is a racist hate group—a band of "Hispanic supremacists," if you will, though it is seldom characterized that way. It is no more a civil rights group than the Ku Klux Klan is a group promoting the civil rights of white people. It is no more a civil rights group than the neo-Nazi scum who marched a generation ago at Skokie, Illinois, with the legal protection of the American Civil Liberties Union, another misnamed organization. It is no more a civil rights group than the Aryan skinheads who victimize Jews and others they detest in trying to lift themselves up from the gutter.

It's not a civil rights group. It's a civil wrongs group.

La Raza is part of the movement in this country to destroy it from within by dividing and "reconquering."

Its members and leadership are linked directly to those who believe the Southwestern United States was unjustly seized from Mexico in the nineteenth century. It should, they believe, by any means necessary, be reconstituted either as part of that thoroughly corrupt, socialist regime fled by tens of millions of refugees or as an independent, autonomous, Spanish-speaking socialist state—like the mythical land of Aztlan.[3]

A review of all their respective literature indicates that the only real differences between La Raza and the neo-Nazis and the KKK appears to be wealth, power, and level of sophistication.

For decades now, Democratic Party politicians have pandered to groups like La Raza in search of constituencies— votes. That is to be expected, given the history of the Democratic Party, the party of the Klan and Jim Crow racism and, yes, even slavery. The Democratic Party is the party of division—the party of group rights rather than individual rights. It is the plantation party that rewards special interests rather than protecting the sovereignty of the individual with unalienable rights bestowed by our Creator.

So, it's business as usual when Democratic Party politicians pay homage to La Raza—and even coercively and unconstitutionally transfer taxpayer wealth to its coffers. (Yes, La Raza is a beneficiary of Washington's largesse with your money!)

But when Republican politicians play this game, it leaves Americans without any viable political alternative. I don't know about you, but I'm not going to drink that Kool-Aid anymore.

John McCain has illustrated, once again, he has crossed over to the dark side. His candidacy as the presumptive Republican presidential nominee does not represent a meaningful choice for Americans committed to the principles of the Declaration of Independence and the Constitution—not by a long shot.

Anyone who believes McCain is telling the truth now when he says he is committed to border security is just plain out of touch with reality.

Like so many disingenuous politicians, John McCain is a chameleon. When he speaks to conservative audiences, he tells them what they want to hear. When he speaks to radical, arguably anti-American groups like La Raza, he tells them what they want to hear.

If you make your political calculations based on what politicians tell you, you are being hosed—plain and simple. Judge them by their fruits. Judge them by their deeds. Judge them by their actions.

By the way, just in case you think McCain only pulled the La Raza stunt as an election gambit, consider this: he also delivered the keynote address to the group's convention in 2004 and received an award from the organization in 1999.[4]

While McCain has been pandering to extremist groups like La Raza for at least a decade, he has demonstrated he will throw overboard even enthusiastic supporters of his campaign and political agenda who are mainstream Christian evangelical leaders who take positions in line with biblical truth.

No, I'm not talking about controversial Texas pastor John Hagee, whose endorsement of McCain was rejected by the candidate when some of his past sermons were scrutinized publicly. At the same time McCain was running away from Hagee, he also dumped an endorsement from Rod Parsley for expressing a standard, biblical Christian viewpoint about Islam.

Parsley, pastor of the World Harvest Church of Columbus, stands accused of calling Islam an "anti-Christ religion."[5] He is also quoted as saying he would like to see "this false religion [Islam] destroyed."[6] He also described Islam's prophet Muhammad as "the mouthpiece of a conspiracy of spiritual evil."[7]

To which I say: "Yeah, where's the controversy?"

I, too, am a Christian who believes in the Bible. And the Bible tells me that all religions not biblically based are false religions and anti-Christ religions that need to be destroyed.

That's not to say we believe in destroying the human beings who practice those faiths. Christians seek to convert Muslims to Christianity by sharing the Gospel of love and forgiveness, just as they seek to convert through loving persuasion all other non-Christians.

As to Muhammad being "the mouthpiece of a conspiracy of spiritual evil," I would have to agree again. All false religions, by definition, are evil to biblical Christians. That's what the Bible says.

Do I expect McCain to get this? No, I don't. And the reason is that McCain doesn't have any faith at all. How could he possibly understand Parsley's passionate expression of a heartfelt belief of mainstream evangelical Christianity?

If McCain is willing to throw Parsley under the train, is he willing to do the same with everyone who agrees with Parsley? Is he willing to forsake every other conservative Christian pastor who understands the Bible states there is only one path and that it comes through God's Son, Jesus Christ?

I think the answer to that question is an unequivocal yes.

Jesus Himself proclaimed it in John 14:6: "I am the way, the truth, and the life: no man cometh unto the Father, but by me."

Just so there is no confusion, Jesus also proclaimed in Matthew 12:30: "He that is not with me is against me; and he that gathereth not with me scattereth abroad."

I'm sure this is all Greek to McCain. But if he is going to welcome support only by people who are ready to proclaim Islam as a viable path to finding God, he is going to find himself very lonely on Election Day.

But what about judges, you ask? Won't a McCain presidency give Americans a chance to reclaim the Supreme Court in the name of the Constitution and original intent?

The evidence is far from conclusive, given that McCain voted to confirm Ruth Bader Ginsburg and Stephen Breyer to the Supreme Court. He also, as is his nature, conspired with Democrats in the Senate to block approval of Bush's most conservative jurists, as noted above. McCain wasn't just a member of the notorious Gang of 14 senators who did this; he was one of the central organizers.

He gave us McCain-Feingold—the worst legislative attack on the First Amendment in decades. This law actually restricts political speech prior to elections—a clearly unconstitutional approach to so-called campaign finance reform.

Most people's eyes glaze over when they hear or read terms like "campaign finance reform."

It's understandable. Many Americans cannot see how this kind of legislation impacts their lives—how it restricts their most fundamental freedoms.

And, accordingly, there was little outrage when Congress passed the McCain-Feingold campaign finance bill.

Again, there was little outrage when President Bush signed the legislation.

Then, in 2003, the Supreme Court ruled 5-4 to uphold the law's ban on so-called soft money, or unlimited donations to political parties, as well as new restrictions on political advertising sixty days before elections.

But this legislation, shockingly upheld by the Court, represents one of the biggest attacks on First Amendment freedoms in America's history.

It's no exaggeration to say Congress, the president, and the court killed freedom of speech with their actions. It all started with Sen. John McCain.

Why?

Because if Congress does indeed have the power to regulate political speech in America—in stark contradiction to what the First Amendment clearly states—then it is only a matter of time and opportunity before the government takes the next step. It is only a matter of time and opportunity before the government takes yet another "privilege" of expression away from the American people, who clearly have no inalienable rights in this area, despite what the Constitution says. It is only a matter of time before Congress eviscerates other provisions of the First Amendment—once considered sacrosanct even by judicial activists who had no use for the rest of the Constitution.

Let's say I, Joe American, want to make my voice heard in opposition to a congressional candidate in my district fifty-nine days before the election. I believe there is a compelling reason to reject a particular candidate—and no one in the media is willing to examine my pet cause. Even the opposing candidate is missing the boat—either through ignorance or oversight.

So, I decide to take out a small ad in my local newspaper—on my own initiative and with my own meager financial resources.

Do you know this wholesome, perfectly appropriate, civic-minded action is illegal under the new law?

Let me give you another real-life example.

Have you ever thought about using your Web site to campaign for your favorite candidate? Or, perhaps, to urge the defeat of that congressional representative who has been ignoring your letters?

Better think again.

A few years ago, Leo Smith of Connecticut decided he would use his business Web site to do just that—urge the defeat of his congressional representative, Republican Nancy L. Johnson. He decided to add a new section to an already existing Internet site to advance the cause of her challenger, Charlotte Koskoff.

Just a few days later, Smith was contacted by Koskoff's campaign manager. No, it wasn't a call to thank him for his efforts. It was a warning of legal problems he might encounter because of campaign finance regulations.

Smith was told by the Federal Election Commission that he was in violation of federal law because he had spent more than $250 in expressing his political views without disclosing his identity and filing the required reports.

Never mind that Smith didn't spend anything (except time) creating the new page. The FEC, however, insisted in an advisory opinion that the value of the computer hardware and software is factored into its calculations. If a computer used to express political viewpoints cost more than $250, the FEC said, its owner would have to meet the filing requirements.[8]

Again, this is before the latest heinous legislation.

The answer to those who say we need stricter limits on campaign spending is that we need *no* limits. Any limits are limits on speech. You cannot divide money and speech. Money buys speech. Effective communication requires money. It's an illusion to pretend otherwise.

And who aided McCain in this successful effort to undermine our Constitution? You might be surprised to learn it was George Soros, the socialist extremist bankrolling Barack Obama's campaign. He also got help from Teresa Heinz Kerry.

WorldNetDaily's Jerome Corsi reported that:

> McCain founded the Alexandria, Virginia-based Reform Institute in 2001 as a vehicle to receive funding from George Soros's Open Society Institute and Teresa Heinz Kerry's Tides

Foundation and several other prominent non-profit organizations. McCain used the institute to promote his political agenda and provide compensation to key campaign operatives between elections.

To this day, the Reform Institute still employs the McCain campaign's Hispanic outreach director, Juan Hernandez, as a senior fellow of its Comprehensive Immigration Reform Initiative.

Prominent senior officials on the McCain 2008 presidential campaign staff found generously paid positions at the Reform Institute following the senator's unsuccessful run for the White House in 2000, Corsi reported in February, 2008.[9] There seems to be a revolving door between the Reform Institute and McCain political campaigns:

Rick Davis, McCain's current campaign manager, was paid $110,000 a year by the Reform Institute for a consulting position, according to the group's 2003 Form 990 filing with the IRS. In 2004, Davis advanced to the position of Reform Institute president, with an annual salary of $120,000, according to the group's 2004 Form 990. In 2005, Davis remained president, but his salary dropped back to $45,000 a year, with a time commitment of five hours per week, according to the 2005 Form 990.

Carla Eudy, a senior advisor on McCain's 2008 presidential campaign who until recently headed fundraising, was paid $177,885 in 2005 to serve as the Reform Institute's secretary-treasurer.

Other McCain presidential campaign staffers who have found employment at the Reform Institute include Trevor Potter, McCain's 2000 legal counsel, and Crystal Benton, the senator's former press secretary, who served as the institute's communications director in 2005 for an annual salary of $52,083."[10]

In addition, the Soros-funded Reform Institute regularly has supported McCain in various legislative efforts, including on campaign finance reform, global warming, and "comprehensive immigration reform."

Soros, who campaigned so hard against Bush in 2000 and 2004, seems to have the best of both worlds in 2008—two major-party candidates beholden to him.

No one is more responsible for that hideously unconstitutional McCain-Feingold legislation than John McCain—not even Soros. We don't need more government control—whether it is through taxpayer-financed elections or limits on political speech. Either solution spells less freedom.

What we need to do, as much as possible, is to get government's nose out of the election process—and, for that matter, the rest of our public and private affairs.

John McCain does not understand this. He does not agree with this. He has a problem with the First Amendment—and other parts of the Constitution.

He's a globalist—standing strong even today behind agreements like the North American Free Trade Agreement that are ravaging Third World economies, eliminating jobs in the United States, and chipping away at U.S. sovereignty and the power of the people. He supported ratification of the Law of the Sea Treaty, which will place under the jurisdiction of the United Nations most of the planet's oceans.

I could go on and on. McCain is wrong on so many issues of the day. But there is one more I feel compelled to share. Some people suggest we should forget all our beefs with McCain and support him because he's right on the war against terrorism. I disagree.

I disagree not only that the issue supersedes all others, but also with the assumption that McCain is right about the conduct of the war.

Need I remind everyone it was John McCain who nearly single-handedly stripped our troops of the interrogation tools they needed to defeat the enemy and prevent attacks on innocent Iraqis and our own soldiers? More than anyone else in American politics, McCain led the fight to stop coercive interrogations, an absolutely essential weapon in our arsenal in the conduct of this war and future wars.

McCain calls it torture. But it is not. Coercive interrogations are a necessity in any successful war campaign. When he stopped them with his legislative campaign, his actions not only prolonged the war and led to higher casualties for American troops and innocent Iraqis, they also ensured any future war will be far more costly in U.S. lives.

How bad would McCain be?

I'll put it this way: worse than Bush.

Are you ready for that?

I'm not.

All things being equal, I'd rather watch the Democrats destroy America for the next four years, holding out hope that a new kind of Republican leadership might arise to fight back in 2012. But I'm not holding my breath.

What I *know* is that it is time for Americans to stop settling for the lowest common denominator in leadership. What I *know* is that reconciling ourselves to voting for the lesser of two evils every election year is not moving this country forward. What I *know* is that John McCain would take the country down essentially the same road as Barack Obama, albeit, perhaps, at a slightly slower speed.

Should the question Americans ask themselves before going into the voting booth in 2008 be, How quickly do I want to see America's most precious values and heritage destroyed?

I don't think that's a good question. Yet, it is the question Americans will face if they are committed to voting for one of the two major-party candidates.

The idea of McCain's finger on the nuclear trigger brings shudders to my very soul. The man is emotionally and psychologically unstable, in my opinion. He is known for outrageous outbursts and public expressions of anger.

Imagining McCain as president brings to mind equally scary and morally repulsive figures—Hillary Clinton, Captain Queeg, and Charles Logan, the fictional president in season five of 24.

Some of my very best friends will argue the point with me. They say McCain is the only choice we have because of national security. We are in a global fight with a desperate and ruthless enemy. This is no time for capitulation and surrender, which is what we will get with an Obama presidency and a Democratic Congress.

But, again, we must fully explore the alternative. Is John McCain committed to absolute victory over our enemies? Or is he committed to an endless war strategy—one that bleeds America slowly and never achieves its objectives?

I take a backseat to no one in my support of the mission to overthrow Saddam Hussein.

I take a backseat to no one in my support of our troops in Iraq.

I take a backseat to no one in my support of a national policy of defeating the number one foreign threat to our national security today—Islamo-fascism.

However, when I hear John McCain justifying and rationalizing and modifying his statement that U.S. troops might need to stay in Iraq for a hundred years, I say the guy should have his head examined.

Not only was this an extremely impolitic remark for a Republican presidential candidate to make, it is downright ridiculous, foolish, wrong.

In fact, despite my own hard-line credentials, given the choice between keeping troops in Iraq for a hundred years or pulling out right now, I would have to opt for the immediate pullout.

We can't stay in Iraq for a hundred years.

And we can't withdraw immediately—not without severe dislocation, chaos, and death.

But we do need to find a sensible exit strategy—the sooner the better.

We don't want Iraq to fall into chaos and civil war. But we can't protect Iraq from Iraqis for another century, either. We shouldn't stay in Iraq one day longer than necessary. It's not good for the United States, and it's not good for Iraq.

It's time to kill the bad guys and get out. This is not the John McCain strategy—make no mistake about it.

McCain will say his words were distorted, misunderstood, taken out of context. They weren't. And that's the most disturbing part of the controversy.

The comment was made in New Hampshire in response to a question by a student who asked about President Bush's remark that U.S. troops might need to remain in Iraq for fifty years.

"Maybe one hundred," McCain chimed in. "As long as Americans are not being injured or harmed or wounded or killed, it's fine with me, and I hope it would be fine with you, if we maintain a presence in a very volatile part of the world where al-Qaida is training, recruiting, equipping, and motivating people every single day."[11]

That's what he said. Nobody put the words in his mouth. And his explanation and rationalization for his comment doesn't make me feel any better about it.

"Of course, that comment of mine was distorted," said McCain. "Life isn't fair, as Jack Kennedy said. I was talking about American presence after the war."[12]

After the war, during the war—Americans do not have to be in Iraq for one hundred years. Period. End of story. Americans will not accept it. Americans should not accept it.

McCain continued: "No American argues against our military presence in Korea or Japan or Germany or Kuwait or other places, or Turkey, because America is not receiving casualties."[13]

Again, I take issue. No American argues with our military presence in Korea, Japan, or Germany? I argue with it. From what are we protecting Germany today? The Soviet Union is gone. It has been gone for more than fifteen years. Had we sought victory in Korea, rather than appeasement, our troops would have been out of that country fifty years ago.

These kinds of endless missions should hardly be our model for military engagements in the future. We cannot and should not be the world's policeman. We cannot occupy the entire world—unless we want to go the way of Rome.

It almost sounds like McCain is looking for a reason to stay in Iraq.

It almost sounds as if he thinks it's a good idea to stay in Iraq.

If he wants to ensure he loses the presidential election by a landslide, he's saying exactly the right thing.

We have been at war in Iraq now for five years. For those arithmetically or historically challenged, that's longer than America's involvement in World War II.

That's too long already. If we could defeat the Nazi war machine and imperial Japan in that time, why can't we defeat the ragtag forces supported by Iran and Syria?

John McCain actually played a significant role in ensuring that this war would not be won quickly. He is the architect of a policy that lengthened the fight and resulted in more death and mayhem.

What am I talking about?

Let me put this simply: the U.S. military doesn't torture prisoners.

Yet, thanks to Sen. John McCain and a few other weak-kneed politicians in the U.S. Senate, we falsely admitted the military *does* torture prisoners to the people of the United States, the people of the world, and, of course, to all our enemies, who effectively used that propaganda against us.

What McCain did was equate what the U.S. military calls coercive interrogations with torture. Because of John McCain, the U.S. military no longer conducts coercive interrogations—procedures vitally necessary to the national security of the United States and to ensuring victory over our Islamo-fascist enemies.

Torture to me means blinding, disfigurement, inflicting cruel and unusual pain, doing permanent harm to a captive. The U.S. military doesn't do that and never has—certainly not as a matter of policy.

But when the politicians and people around the world saw the pictures from Abu Ghraib, showing prisoners with panties on their heads, the rules on interrogations became more strict. You may like that. You may feel good about that. But those new rules make no sense and are costing the lives of American soldiers and Iraqi civilians, and may someday cost the lives of U.S. civilians, as well.

What these new rules mean in the battlefield is that no human intelligence is forthcoming from prisoners. None. Zip. Zilch. Nada.

In the early stages of the Afghan and Iraq campaigns, massive amounts of human intelligence were derived from coercive interrogations. That flow of information has stopped. It stopped when John McCain got his way.

What is being characterized as torture now are such techniques as sleep deprivation, diet management, and stress positions. They do not result in death. They do not result in permanent scarring or injury. But they do result in prisoners talking—nearly 100 percent of the time.

Why is it that we seem to have no problem sending combat units out to kill, maim, and mutilate the enemy, but we get squeamish when we see pictures of grown men with panties on their heads?

Why is it that we have no moral qualms with bombing raids that kill indiscriminately, but we get upset about terrorists deprived of sleep?

Why is it that we tolerate the constant stream of attacks on U.S. troops and Iraqi civilians, but we won't reconsider using the tried-and-true methods of coercive interrogations that can prevent them and bring these wars to speedier conclusions?

Why is it that we train our own soldiers to endure such techniques but refuse to use them in spite of their effectiveness in achieving victory and preventing attacks on our forces and our friends?

This background is necessary to understand what John McCain has done in the last four years—prolonged our wars, aided the enemy with invaluable propaganda, turned the world against the United States for something it is not doing, and cost civilian and military lives.

Effective interrogation techniques have already been disallowed. Our troops cannot achieve victory with these handcuffs placed on them. They should be turned loose so they can get the job done and come home.

The U.S. military impressed Iraqis, impressed the world, and impressed our enemies in the early stages of the war with what we called "shock and awe." Yet we now have senators and armchair generals who think intimidating a terrorist is immoral.

"The bottom line? When U.S. forces catch a bomber and cannot find out where his supplier is, who the financer is, or where other bombs are, soldiers die," a veteran interrogator told me. "However, in most cases nowadays, it is innocent Iraqi men, women, and children who die horrible deaths by bombing, execution-style shootings, or beheadings. Another consideration: When the U.S. military doesn't know where or who exactly the terrorists are, it uses bombs—which means collateral damage and much more innocent carnage."

He continues: "Some lawyers believe that U.S. interrogation techniques are morally wrong. But if these men and women saw real war footage of what a .50-caliber machine gun does to a man, most would likely reconsider how egregious it is to put panties on a prisoner's head."

Americans are simply losing their ability to distinguish right from wrong.

I don't know how else to put it.

Up is down, day is night, left is right, and right is wrong.

A good illustration of my thesis is the growing political consensus around the idea that the United States should stop using any effective interrogation techniques that make our terrorist enemies—even those involved in planning acts of mass destruction and annihilation—uncomfortable.

For instance, armchair generals are increasingly referring to "waterboarding" as torture and saying it must be stopped in all cases.

I have no doubts waterboarding is a very unpleasant experience. It must be so because it is considered 100 percent effective and usually induces cooperation within thirty seconds.

The technique of waterboarding involves pouring water on the head of a prisoner with the purpose of triggering a gagging reflex and the panic of imminent drowning.

It was used successfully to learn about terrorist operations planned by two of al-Qaida's top operatives—Khalid Sheikh Mohammed, involved in the planning of the 9/11 attack, and Abu Zubaida, another leader of the terrorist organization.

Apparently both of these mass killers endured many hours of coercive interrogations without talking. But they sang like canaries after a few seconds of waterboarding.

In both cases, there is reason to believe planned terrorist attacks were foiled as a result of this technique.

Nevertheless, there is a growing chorus of opposition against any further use of waterboarding in similar or even more dire scenarios.

Let's use our heads for a minute.

Imagine American law enforcement or military authorities have captured a terrorist mastermind who has knowledge about an imminent nuclear detonation in an unknown American city. He knows the time, the location, and the details about the warhead.

The bomb could be going off at any minute. It could kill hundreds of thousands of innocent people.

Would you really want waterboarding to be banned under all circumstances? What alternatives would you suggest for quick results? Should we call in top negotiators from the State Department? Should we play loud rap music? Should we force the prisoner to listen to Barack Obama campaign speeches?

While I also find those experiences unpleasant, I don't think they would produce the needed results in time to defuse the bomb.

Let's not tie the hands of future Jack Bauers who will need to do what they have to do to save lives.

I personally think Mohammed and Zubaida got off way too easy with waterboarding.

I would personally have performed far more unpleasant procedures on them without a twinge of guilt in my conscience. Real torture techniques would have been appropriate in both cases.

But here's why waterboarding is not torture.

Do you know the U.S. military waterboards hundreds of our own soldiers every year? It is part of the conditioning Special Forces troops undergo to prepare for battle and the possibility of capture by the enemy.

In other words, it's okay for us to do this to America's best and brightest, but it's too horrible for our worst enemies?

Does this make sense to anyone?

Many Americans are simply confused about the real definition of torture. Since so little sacrifice is required of most Americans today and because so few have ever experienced combat, they equate momentary discomfort or fear with torture. They are not the same.

My definition of torture is simple: it involves physical or mental abuse that leaves lasting scars. Cutting off fingers, toes, limbs—that would be torture. Forcing prisoners to play

Russian roulette—that would be torture. Sticking hot pokers in the eyes of prisoners—that would be torture.

But a few seconds of dripping water on a prisoner's face? That's not torture to me.

John McCain told Americans we had to ban coercive interrogation techniques—what he calls "torture"—because our enemies would use them against U.S. captives.

Well, guess what?

We banned the most effective tool in our arsenal for gathering intelligence on our enemy's plans in Iraq, and al-Qaida is still inventing gruesome torture techniques that would make Hannibal Lecter blush.

Just to set the record straight, the United States never countenanced what most of us think of as torture—the kinds of techniques, for instance, regularly employed by Jack Bauer on 24.

Here are some of the real-life "abuses" found to have taken place at Guantanamo Bay and Abu Ghraib:

- Wrestling thrashing, spitting detainee to the ground after he head butted an MP (military policeman)

- Telling a detainee no one loved, cared for, or remembered him

- Placing a smiley-face mask made from an MRE (meals ready to eat) box over a detainee's face for a few moments after telling him how ungrateful and grumpy he was

- Conducting a puppet show satirizing a detainee's involvement with al-Qaida

- Waking a detainee with Christina Aguilera music

- Making a prisoner stand for the playing of the American national anthem

With the possible exception of using Christina Aguilera music for reveille, I don't find any of these practices particularly abusive. Do you?

Yet it is precisely this kind of technique that has been banned by the U.S. Congress as TORTURE!

That law, sponsored by McCain, has been one of the central reasons momentum in the war on Iraq shifted to the enemy. Before military policy on coercive interrogations was changed, we were getting information from captives. Since the change, no information is provided because prisoners know the limits of their captors. They've been spelled out publicly for them!

Among the other heinous abuses outlawed by the McCain bill are the following:

- Forcing prisoners to stand for prolonged periods

- Isolating terrorists for up to thirty days

- Removing prisoners' clothing

- Forced shaving of facial hair

- Playing on "individual phobias" (such as dogs)

- "Mild, non-injurious physical contact" such as grabbing, poking in the cheek with a finger, light pushing

- Use of wet towels or dripping water to induce misperception of suffocation (waterboarding)

- Longer interrogation sessions

- Dripping water over the head to arouse from sleep

Now let's take a look at what our enemy is doing—even though we have banned all of the above. A newly released al-

Qaida manual on coercive interrogations shows the principal adversary in Iraq encouraging the following:

- Dragging captives behind a moving car or truck
- Amputating limbs with meat cleavers
- Using blowtorches on human skin
- Extracting eyes with sharp tools
- Cracking skulls in a vise
- Using power drills on human hands
- Suspending captives with ropes from ceilings

You see, al-Qaida is fighting this war with one objective in mind—total victory. The United States is fighting this war with a mind toward popularity around the world.

I will leave it to you to determine which course is proving more effective.

Am I suggesting we should resort to the tactics of the enemy?

Absolutely not! We shouldn't—and we never have. But, please, examine the coercive techniques (not torture) we outlawed and compare them with the coercive techniques (REAL torture) being used by al-Qaida.

The enemy will get the information it is looking for. We will not. It's just that simple.

Time alone is not what brings victory. Seeking victory is what brings victory.

Unless we clearly define victory and seek it relentlessly and ferociously at all costs, it will elude us, and the war against terrorism will end badly for Iraq, for the United States, and for the world.

The United States is not an empire. Americans don't seek to dominate other countries or peoples. We want only freedom for others and security for ourselves. Those are the goals we had in Iraq and they should remain the goals—the definition of "mission accomplished."

Achieving those goals requires us to take the handcuffs off our military and a ruthless strategy of attacking and destroying the enemy wherever he hides—even in a neighboring country. If we are not prepared for that kind of all-out war, indeed, we should never have entered the battlefield. That's the nature of war.

I'm reminded of the bad choices we have before us— surrender or a one-hundred-year, low-intensity war—by a recent poll taken in South Korea.

It shows 34 percent of first-year army cadets in South Korea see the United States as their main enemy.

Kim Choong-bae, president of the Korea Institute for Defense Analyses, disclosed the results of the survey of 250 army cadets. He said, "While the majority [sic]—or 34 percent—picked the U.S., 33 percent said they regarded North Korea as the main enemy." He said the result was unbelievable, stressing the respondents were those who were supposed to be military officers.

Kim hinted that he had been asked not to notify the public of the result. He blames the country's schools, which do not portray the U.S. in a positive light.

Another survey of conscripted soldiers conducted by the Ministry of Defense found about 75 percent of them said they have anti-United States sentiment. Others taken in high schools and colleges offered similar anti-American perceptions.[14]

That's the cost of prolonged occupation—even when it is for the best of purposes, like protecting the lives of innocent people from military aggression, protecting freedom, and making the world a safer place.

We must never measure military and political success by the lengths of our military engagements. We should measure them by the brevity of our military engagements.

John McCain may indeed win the presidency. But it won't be because he is in tune with the will of the American people. It will be because they don't really know John McCain's record and because the Democratic Party will be split over the fractious primary campaign between Hillary Clinton and Barack Obama.

But John McCain won't get any help from me. He won't get my vote. In fact, to be honest, if the Republican Party is ever going to recover itself and become the party it was under Ronald Reagan, it will happen faster if John McCain is beaten. It will happen faster if Barack Obama gets elected and implements the Big Brother, socialist agenda he endorses.

Bring it on. I'll do my best to expose it. Maybe the American people will wake up and rediscover the meaning of freedom after tasting elitist, top-down, command-and-control, centralized socialism.

We're all going to experience it in the next four years. It's simply a question of who is going to be force-feeding it to us. I'd rather it come from the Democrats, so the American people know whom to blame.

There is no question in my mind that if Barack Obama sits in the White House for the next four years, especially with the backing of a Democratic Congress, he will put in place policies that will anger Americans.

He will set the stage for his own undoing. He will have nothing to complain about anymore. He will have all the levers of power at his disposal. He will have no excuses. He will be forced to create the panacea he has been promising for so long.

And, of course, he will fail.

His ideas simply don't work. They create misery, not prosperity. They create strife, not unity. They make war, not peace.

If the Democrats have all the cards, as they last did briefly in 1993 and 1994, they will overreach, and the American people will know whom to blame.

On the other hand, if John McCain wins, he will institute most of the same policy prescriptions. He will steal your money to fight phantom problems like "global warming." He will do away with tax cuts he opposed in the first place. He will approve federal funding of embryonic stem cell research. He will promote amnesty for illegal aliens. He will sign legislation attacking constitutionally protected political speech. He will nominate judges who will get the easy approval of the Democrats in the Senate.

It's really difficult for me to see significant substantive difference between McCain and Obama.

While it is true McCain would continue the war in Iraq, he has already assured that our troops in this war and future wars, as well as in the current conflict in Afghanistan, will be handcuffed by rules of engagement dictated by politicians who simply have no comprehension of the kinds of enemies we face. And McCain will be content to occupy, without total victory, for a hundred years, as he suggested.

In other words, Americans lose no matter who wins in November.

Some Republicans make the case that *not* voting for McCain makes a Barack Obama victory more likely. However, I say there is actually more hope for positive change in the short term with a Democratic sweep—not that I advocate actively pulling the lever for Obama.

Here's the difference: Democrats will finally get the chance to conduct their diabolical social experiment on America without restraint if they hold on to Congress and take the White House. It won't take long for Americans to see the error of their ways. We last saw it between 1976 and 1980. What followed was the most glorious political revolution of the twentieth century under the leadership of Ronald Reagan.

Even though McCain will cause nearly as much short-term pain as Obama, Americans will be confused about why. They won't know whom to blame. Democrats will surely blame McCain—the only Republican in their way. And a

McCain presidency is more likely to lead to a Democratic White House in 2012.

Further, if McCain wins, he will spend the next four years insisting it was his maverick brand of Republicanism—his willingness "to reach across the aisle" and find compromise and common ground—that led to victory for the GOP. Who will be able to argue effectively against that idea?

No, I won't be a part of that scenario. McCain could well beat Obama without any help from freedom-minded Americans who stick to their guns when it comes to the Constitution. They are both deeply flawed candidates. But he will get no help from me. I honestly believe America will be better off taking its medicine now—delivered by a clearly identifiable "progressive" like Obama.

That could set the stage for the emergence of another grand revolution like we experienced in 1980. McCain, on the other hand, would likely lead America into forty years in the political wilderness—or maybe one hundred years in Iraq.

And it should not be forgotten that McCain's hero, indeed his obsession, is Theodore Roosevelt—hardly a paragon of limited government.[15] But this shouldn't surprise anyone. In 2004, McCain reportedly seriously entertained joining John Kerry as the vice presidential nominee.[16] In the span of four years, how can a man go from almost being on the Democratic ticket to being on the Republican ticket?

For anyone else, this would be impossible. But not for John McCain. Why? Because John McCain is a Democrat. And Republican voters should remember that this November.

CHAPTER FIVE

THE PROBLEM WITH THE REPUBLICAN PARTY

*I*MAGINE for a moment that Republicans were to win every single House seat on Election Day.

Go a step further and pretend the GOP was to take every Senate seat that is up for grabs.

I suspect there are many reading this book who believe this would be a development rivaled in significance perhaps only by the Second Coming.

No doubt it would mean an improvement in the way the federal government operates. I wouldn't argue that point. It would probably mean tax cuts. And tax cuts are good. It might even mean some downsizing of government in general. And downsizing government is always good.

But would it herald a return to constitutional government?

I don't think so.

Too many Republicans don't honor the Constitution any more than their Democratic counterparts. They don't understand the federal government is strictly limited by the Constitution in its powers. They don't understand that most lawmaking authority was reserved by our wise founders for the states. They don't understand that the great American experiment in politics was its commitment to self-government—meaning a commitment to individual liberty and responsibility. They don't even understand the concept of self-government.

Of course, the Republicans won't win all the marbles in November—not even close. In fact, in all likelihood, they will lose seats in both houses—probably many.

While I am not a registered Republican, there is no question the philosophy of the Republican Party is better than that of the Democratic Party. It is less evil. It is less immoral. The problem is that too many Republican politicians—most, in fact—simply don't live up to Republican ideals. More importantly, they don't honor and respect the U.S. Constitution, which is much more important than the Republican platform.

Remember the 1994 "Contract with America"? It was seen as a high-water mark for the party in many ways. But Republicans need to understand we already have a contract with America—the Constitution.

For those hoping for a revolution at the ballot box—one that would return America to a moral and constitutional foundation of self-government in which the rule of law and godly worldview reign supreme—you are misplacing your hope. It's not going to happen in 2008. There would first need to be transformation of one of the two major parties or the creation of a new viable third party for that to be even a remote possibility.

The battle to expand freedom cannot be achieved at the ballot box alone. The battle to restore America's commitment to self-government will not happen as a result of political campaigns alone. The battle to return America to its revolutionary founding principles will not happen because of the election of Republicans, Libertarians, or any other politicians alone. It won't happen because of a "contract with America."

It will happen because the American people get serious about the Constitution.

This year marks the fourteenth anniversary of the "Republican Revolution" of 1994.

That's when Republicans took control of the House and Senate for a time. They finally lost both houses of Congress in 2006 and hold on to the presidency with a tenuous grasp. What did the Republicans accomplish during their time in power?

Even when they had control, at least in theory, of all three branches of the federal government, it was difficult to perceive any significant positive change in course for the nation. Spending went way up—even if you don't consider the expenses of the war in Iraq and Afghanistan. Seven years after America was the target of a devastating, unthinkable terrorist attack, the borders remain unsecured.

Somehow Republicans have managed to squander every advantage they had fourteen years ago as "mavericks" who were going to make government more accountable to the people, less corrupt, responsive to the rule of law, more moral.

It hasn't happened. That's obvious to one and all—even the most hopeful of us. The Republican Party is clearly part of the problem. A significant portion of the GOP base now recognizes, rightly, that no fundamental change in the direction of the country will occur because of the election of Republicans to office—even if they occupied every single seat in the House, Senate, and Supreme Court and the White House.

"Republican" no longer connotes smaller government, more freedom, less intrusion into our personal lives, and a more vibrant economy, as it did after eight years of Ronald Reagan. "Republican" today more likely connotes—even for those who tend to vote for the party—incompetence, corruption, compromise, betrayal.

None of this, of course, is to excuse or rationalize the Democratic Party as a viable alternative. That would be like rejecting the frying pan for the fire.

But, nevertheless, think what will happen on Election Day when 2 to 3 percent of the previously most passionate "Republicans" stay home. Think of what it will mean when 20 to 30 percent of the grassroots activists Republicans have counted on to work for them don't show up this year.

That's what I expect to happen in 2008.

I expect the Democrats to make tremendous gains in the House and Senate by default—simply because the Republicans have blown it over the last fourteen years. They have not distinguished themselves as a better alternative.

In fact, they have squandered the greatest historic opportunity to rein in unconstitutional government in Washington since the War Between the States. And they don't deserve to be rewarded for it.

Today, the party leadership shows no signs of "getting it." They have put personality above principle—and there is no chance of going back, at least not without a major wake-up call. I say 2008 is the year to give it to them.

Just as the party leadership doesn't get it, neither do most of the people of the United States. That makes it even more important for those who do to deliver that wake-up call. The country is not ready for that second American revolution. Not yet. It needs one. But the people don't know it. And, even if they did, there is no party mechanism representing such an expression of popular will.

What America needs first is a spiritual awakening—the kind of revival that preceded the War of Independence in the eighteenth century. Spiritual awakening leads to moral renewal, and moral renewal leads to self-government, limited government, freedom.

You can't have the latter without the former.

That's why you can't count on ballot-box revolutions. America is not a country currently capable of true self-government. It's become a nation of people looking for handouts. It's become a nation of people coveting their neighbor's property. It's become a nation governed more by coercion than by conscience.

Real progress never comes easily. It involves sacrifice. It involves pain.

I hope and pray that Americans reacquire their taste for freedom. I hope and pray they reacquire the tools they need to appreciate it and practice it. I hope and pray Americans reacquire the knowledge and wisdom necessary to understand from where their rights descend—not from government, but from God.

It is in this context that the 2008 elections need to be viewed.

The Democratic Party is thoroughly evil and corrupt. And the Republican Party is not a good and healthy alternative. Does that leave Americans with no choice in 2008? No. Does that mean Americans can't express themselves in a historic way that will make a difference in the future? No. Does that mean the Republican Party cannot be redeemed in the future? No.

In fact, I would argue we have a unique opportunity this year to make our voices heard in a new way in American politics by choosing "none of the above."

It's not easy. It's not the whole solution. It's not a quick fix. But it's not the only answer. There's much more work that needs to be done at the same time and for years to come. But I believe it's the right thing and this November is the right time.

For a long time, I have been advocating voters refuse to support any candidate for office who does not acknowledge the supremacy of the U.S. Constitution and the principles of self-governance America established at its founding. America was hardly perfect then. But its birth represented a breakthrough in freedom for the entire world.

It's time to think outside the ballot box. It's time for some radical thinking. It's time to live up to the legacy of our founders.

Voting Republican or Democrat is hardly a way to do that—especially when we are faced with the kind of choices we have in 2008.

Both major parties have such blatant disregard for the concept of limited constitutional government.

Let me give you an example. In 2001, people in New York City who wanted government off their backs cheered when Michael Bloomberg was elected over his opponent, Mark Green. Bloomberg was, after all, "a Republican," who ran to the right of Green.

Yet, it turns out, Bloomberg was actually a lifelong Democrat who merely switched parties to avoid a crowded and difficult primary race.

And, as soon as Bloomberg took office, he showed his true political stripes. One thing he did, for example, was promote a sweeping anti-tobacco bill that banned smoking for the first time in bars, restaurants, bingo parlors, bowling alleys, even private offices.

Now, even among readers of this book, I'm sure there are many anti-smoking zealots who ask what is wrong with such a plan. Simple. It is 100 percent anti-freedom and anti-choice, and a serious blow to private property rights and the free market.

If government has the authority to ban smoking in private offices and in privately owned bars and restaurants, then it has the authority to ban smoking in private homes. In fact, there is nothing government can't do—no right it can't restrict or limit—if it can get away with this. It's tyranny, pure and simple.

No one is forced to be a patron of an establishment where smoking is tolerated. No one. That's the beauty of the free-market system. It allows us to make individual choices. Top-down, command-and-control governance creates a one-size-fits-all system that removes choice, removes freedom.

I don't care if it's the most popular legislation ever written in New York. It is beyond the scope of government's authority to tell private property owners what they can and can't do with their establishments. Without private property rights, we have no rights at all.

But Bloomberg was seen in New York as the lesser of two evils. Many freedom-minded people in New York insisted he was the best leader their city could produce. They suggested things would be worse under Democrat Green.

As I am fond of saying, the lesser of two evils is still evil. Americans must stop this practice if they have any hope of retaining the basic character of American self-governance.

It's time to say no. It's time to resist. It's time to boycott an election fraud that gives us no choice. It's time to raise the standards of political debate in this country. If that means not voting, so be it. If that means voting for a candidate who has little chance of winning, so be it. If that means a write-in, so be it. If that's the price of a clear conscience, it's hardly a price at all. And, I believe, this form of directed non-participatory protest in an evil system may be the only action that can help us take America back.

For those of you looking for political salvation to the "Grand Old Party," it's time to get realistic.

There's not a dime's worth of difference between the Democrats and Republicans.

The nickel's worth of difference between the two major parties can best be summarized as the choice between the express lane and the regular commuter lane of the road paved with good intentions. And you know where that highway leads.

The Democrat-Republican trap is actually little more than a mutual-protection racket for an organized criminal conspiracy of the most dangerous kind. Here's what the modern political paradigm represents:

- Not only the theft and redistribution of actual private property, but a full-scale frontal assault on the whole sacred concept of private property. Thus, the only debate going on in Congress today is over the possibility and propriety of whether legalized confiscation of property should be stepped up or slowed down ever so slightly à la a modest tax cut.

- Invasions of personal privacy that would make the boys in Beijing proud. Government not only decides which pitiful portion of personal property citizens are permitted to keep, it also seeks broader control of how citizens are permitted to use the wealth they have managed to accumulate under the watchful eye of Caesar. We're on the verge of mandatory national ID cards, banking regulations that track even small cash transactions and electronic surveillance of our every move, conversation, and communication.

- The debate over a thoroughly failed government education system never touches on whether it should be scrapped, but focuses instead on how increasing amounts of forcibly confiscated taxpayer money should be spent to perpetuate the dumbing down of the citizenry—making government's "subjects" and "dependents" even more pliable and accepting of control.

The one trump card held by the remnant with enough historical memory to understand that government is supposed to serve rather than be served and be limited in power rather than unlimited—the constitutionally enumerated right to bear arms—has been so narrowly redefined and broadly attacked as to be rendered meaningless. It's simply a matter of time under the Demonicrats and Republicons before it is eliminated and government confiscates all weapons that would pose a threat to its authority and control. The day is coming. Mark my words.

The founders of this once-great country believed that personal freedom could only be realized through self-government—the concept that each individual is responsible for governing himself. When was the last time you heard a

Republican, let alone a Democrat, even use the term "self-government"? It's not even in their limited bureaucratic vocabularies.

Neither is the simple yet profound notion that "Government governs best which governs least."

Some will argue with me, saying that, despite their lack of vision, connection with the Constitution, understanding of America's founding principles, and ability to distinguish themselves from the statist policies of the Democrats, the Republicans represent the lesser of two evils.

My answer: America is too far down the road paved with good intentions to be salvaged by lesser degrees of evil. It's going to take a radical change in course for Americans to rediscover the wonders of freedom, limited government, individual rights, and personal responsibility.

Republican members of the House and Senate are, for the most part, weak-kneed, self-interested, badly misinformed, and incapable of distinguishing right from wrong.

Just for illustration purposes, let me introduce you to the man who may be the dumbest member of Congress.

Who could it be?

Ted Kennedy?

Joe Biden?

Jack Murtha?

I admit it. There's quite a bit of competition for the title.

Could it be Maxine Waters, Barbara Lee, or Patty Murray?

No, I'm not limiting the choices to men of the male persuasion. We're talking about men here in the sense of mankind. These chicks are in contention—no question about it. Each has made her own bid for the honor.

What about Jim Moran?

Charlie Rangel?

Robert Byrd?

It's a tough choice, isn't it? There are lots of qualified candidates.

Could it be Mark Udall?

Or Tom Udall?

Or Anyone Named Udall?

These are all good nominees, without a doubt. But I think there is a clear choice for the title. The only thing that has kept him from earning the title before is his own obscurity—and, perhaps, the fact that he is a Republican.

Do you want to know who I think is the dumbest man in Congress?

It is Sen. George Voinovich (R-OH).

Personally, I came to this conclusion while listening to the man babble and sputter last summer during what should have been a routine interview with radio talker Sean Hannity— friendly to most Republicans.

But Voinovich, being the dumbest man in Congress, self-destructed. He imploded. He self-immolated. He nuked himself.

For starters, Voinovich demonstrated he had no clue what the Fairness Doctrine was. This was pretty strange, given some of his colleagues were clamoring at the time to reinstate the rule that required broadcasters to provide, according to the standards of government bureaucrats, all sides of important policy issues.

"Fairness Doctrine—I'm all for it, whatever it is," he said. "I think everyone should be open to show the other side. That's what you do every night on Fox. That's great!"

When Hannity reminded Voinovich that the Fairness Doctrine would establish government regulatory bureaucracies to enforce this balance, Voinovich quickly retreated. He also completely misinterpreted the results of a vote in the Senate hours earlier.[1]

Let's just say he didn't handle himself real well.

Now let's put this in perspective. Would voting for Voinovich over a Democrat make a meaningful difference for the governance of this country? I don't think so—especially when you consider what's coming down the pike in 2009.

I take a backseat to no one in appreciating the hideousness of what is likely to result from a Democratic sweep in November. Among other things, prepare for a major frontal assault on the First Amendment—perhaps the worst in American history.

To understand what is on the horizon, we need to recall an event from last fall. You might remember an effort by Harry Reid and forty other members of the U.S. Senate who wrote a letter to Rush Limbaugh's network demanding he apologize for something he never said.

It was a brazen power play. Rush acquitted himself well, as he always does—making a monkey out of the Senate majority leader. But if that's all we remember about this incident, we are missing the point.

This was a shot across the bow by an arrogant group of petty, wannabe tyrants who would, if they could, use the coercive power of the state to stifle all dissenting views.

I know because they (the Clintons) came after me back in the 1990s—using the IRS as their attack dog. Many of you will be too young to remember the way the IRS "coincidentally" audited virtually everyone who was critical of the Clintons during their reign of terror. They got away with it—as they got away with so much.

These people, and I mean Democrats, are ruthless, and they are determined to consolidate their power when they get it.

They would do it under the rubric of "hate speech" legislation. They would do it with the rationalization of "fairness" and "accuracy"—two qualities they wouldn't recognize if they tripped over them. They would do it in the name of campaign finance reform. In fact, they would do it without any excuse whatsoever.

Reid and Hillary did us a favor last fall. They tipped the Democrats' hand. They gave us a glimpse of the future under their rule. They told us what they are going to do.

Among other things, they are going to declare war on the First Amendment.

To them, the First Amendment doesn't actually protect the inalienable right to free speech and the free press. It only protects *their* speech and *their* press. They want a monopoly on the media. They had it once and they got spoiled. They decided they can't live without it anymore.

So, here's the plan: come January 2009, if Harry Reid is still running the Senate and Nancy Pelosi is still cleaning the House, they are going to pass a law bringing back the so-called Fairness Doctrine.

If Barack Obama is in the White House, he will sign it. How President John McCain would respond is anyone's guess. Recently, he pledged to oppose it. But let's just say he has a less-than-cordial relationship with talk radio and a history of contempt for the First Amendment.

How draconian would the Fairness Doctrine be?

Would it really make a difference on our media landscape today?

To understand the threat, you have to understand the history of this dreaded, freedom-killing initiative.

In 1987, President Ronald Reagan virtually single-handedly killed the Fairness Doctrine, which, in theory, mandated a balance of opposing views on radio and television airwaves, but, in reality, meant politicians and the government meddling in broadcast programming, resulting in bland, non-controversial shows and the near-death experience of AM radio.

To give you an idea of its chilling effect, in 1987, the last year of the Fairness Doctrine, there were seventy-five radio talk shows in all of these United States. Today, there are over three thousand.

What does that tell you?

Do you think we had more fairness then or now?

Do you think we had more voices then or now?

Do you think we had a more lively political dialogue then or now?

We had an explosion of voices and a livelier and freer debate than ever as a direct result of the Fairness Doctrine being eliminated.

Reid and Pelosi and Obama know that, too. And that's why high on their agenda in 2009 is legislation to bring it back.

They don't want debate. They don't want a multitude of voices. They don't want watchdogs. They want control. They want the media to dance to their tune. They want media lapdogs.

That's what they'll get when they bring back the Fairness Doctrine. And, trust me, the Fairness Doctrine's limits on broadcasters will be only the beginning.

If the Democrats and their me-too Republican allies are successful at sacking talk radio, there will be no stopping them. These are people who actually believe in hate-speech laws. They will be coming after all their enemies—just as they did in the 1990s. There will be no place to hide.

Broadcast will be first. Then they will go after the Internet with taxes and new regulations and hate-crimes laws. And when they succeed at muzzling dissenting voices there, they will even turn to print. Remember, we are dealing with a neo-fascist mentality here. These are people who want the federal government to take over healthcare. These are people who seek to end free enterprise because it promotes global warming. These are people who want to declare another government war on poverty—a war we already fought and lost with their approach back in the 1960s.

We're not dealing with rational, sane human beings here.

Now, why do I worry about what President McCain might do?

Aside from his sponsorship of McCain-Feingold, which, until now, has been the worst legislative attack on the First Amendment and free political speech in the nation's history, the Republicans have a long history of approval of the Fairness Doctrine.

And then we have Republicans in Congress like George Voinovich, who, apparently, doesn't even know what the Fairness Doctrine is or was. Is that an alternative? Is that fighting back? Is that setting America on the right course?

Remember Trent Lott warning last year that something needed to be done about talk radio? Big surprise. He supported making the Fairness Doctrine the law of the land in 1987. He's a *Republican*.

How about Newt Gingrich? He championed legislating the Fairness Doctrine twenty years ago. He's a *Republican*.

Jesse Helms supported it, too. He was a *Republican*.

I know it's hard for many younger Americans to imagine and others to recall that just twenty years ago there was no talk radio, no Internet, no satellite radio, no New Media.

In fact, as I have said before, I know the specific day that New Media was born—and with the birth came an explosion of free expression.

It was August 4, 1987. Something momentous happened on that date. Something wonderful. Something that changed the world for the better.

It was on that date the Federal Communications Commission abolished the Fairness Doctrine by a 4-0 vote.

It was a great day for freedom, liberty, and open and lively political debate.

But, of course, it did not occur in a political vacuum. Two months earlier, on June 19, 1987, another great day for the First Amendment, President Ronald Reagan vetoed a bipartisan bill overwhelmingly approved in both the House and Senate that would have, for the first time, made the Fairness Doctrine a matter of law, not just the guideline of a regulatory agency.

In doing so, Reagan said, "The framers of the First Amendment, confident that public debate would be freer and healthier without the kind of interference represented by the 'Fairness Doctrine,' chose to forbid such regulations in the clearest terms: 'Congress shall make no law...abridging the freedom of speech, or of the press.'"[2]

That took place twenty-one years ago. How many of you remember what the media world looked like two decades ago?

In 1988, three major broadcast networks presented the semi-official newscasts. You could choose between ABC, CBS, and NBC. But there was really no choice at all. All three evening newscasts were remarkably similar—almost as if they were produced by the same team.

There was no talk radio, to speak of, in 1988. The AM dial was moribund. Programmers dared not deal with controversial topics for fear they would have to provide government-mandated "balance" from opposing views. That made for bad programming and lots of red tape and expense. So radio stations simply avoided controversy—sticking to news, traffic, commercial programming, safe stuff. Music had pretty much all moved over to the FM dial.

But something dramatic was right around the corner—a momentous development that would breathe new life into AM radio and the nation's political debate, as well.

President Reagan changed the media landscape for the better with a stroke of the pen. It wasn't executive activism in the negative sense. He was, in fact, restoring constitutional freedoms.

This was not some spontaneous decision on his part. He had been thinking about it for a long time. He had worked in radio and television for much of his life. He had selected members of the FCC who were constitutionalists and freedom-minded people who detested the Fairness Doctrine.

Ronald Reagan should be considered the godfather of the New Media. Two years after he killed the Fairness Doctrine, Rush Limbaugh's nationally syndicated radio talk show took to the airwaves. The impact was phenomenal. Whereas there were some seventy-five talk shows on radio stations across America in 1980, by 1999, there were more than thirteen hundred.

Something else was triggered by the explosion of voices on talk radio—new voices in another medium.

Within eight years of scrapping the Fairness Doctrine and six years of the debut of Rush Limbaugh, another major media voice arose—Matt Drudge. Within two more years— an even decade since the death of the Fairness Doctrine— *WorldNetDaily.com* was born.

Not only did the explosion of new voices affect a broadcast medium once regulated by the Fairness Doctrine, its force carried outside to the Internet, to satellite radio, and to cable TV.

It all started with Ronald Reagan's insightful, inspired stroke of the pen. That's what touched off a media revolution that is far from over twenty years later.

Reagan had to battle Democrats and Republicans— conservatives and liberals. But he won. And he was right.

But, clearly, there are no more Reagans around. Not this year. Not by a long shot.

And the 2009 Congress is going to be more eager to muzzle talk radio than even the current bunch. And not even George W. Bush will be around to stop them.

It's coming.

It's not a threat. It's a promise. It's not a prediction. It is a guarantee.

If the Democrats retain control of both houses of Congress and capture the presidency in 2008, the Fairness Doctrine will be back—this time as the law of the land. Obama would sign it in a flat second.

So, if that's the case, am I making an argument to vote Republican? No. Am I making an argument to get McCain elected on the chance he might veto such an effort? No. Am I making an argument to abandon my "none of the above" recommendation? No.

Instead I am suggesting there is little we can do with many of our affirmative political choices in 2008 to make a difference in blocking such destructive legislation. Obviously, people like

George Voinovich, no matter their party allegiance, will not be allies in the cause of protecting our critical freedoms.

Are there good Republicans out there running for Congress who are outspoken constitutionalists who would stand up to fight against more government intrusion into our lives? Yes, and they should be supported. But don't assume, just because someone places an "R" after their name, they are on the right side, that they get it, that they have the intestinal fortitude to do battle. Don't abandon them. We'll need those allies in the future.

However, as I will explain in chapter seven of this book, there is a positive side effect of casting a negative vote in 2008. Party affiliation is not the answer. Casting truly discerning and discriminating votes is.

We're faced with a profound choice in 2008. We're faced with an opportunity. We can think long term and remake one of the major political parties in our image—the image of self-government, constitutionally limited government, respect for personal responsibility and individual rights. Failing that, we can take the first steps toward creating a viable third party committed to those principles. But we can't do either of these things with a business-as-usual approach to politics.

There's something else wrong with the Republican Party that needs to be addressed. And that is the issue of competence.

Movie producer Robert Evans once put it this way: "Almost all my friends are Democrats, but I am a Republican, for one reason: Ever since I was twelve, I worked and paid Social Security and income taxes, and I always took home more money in my pocket during Republican administrations. They really are the party of the working man, but people don't know it. The Republicans just have the worst sales pitch."[3]

Evans has a point, but it is not one that endears the Republican Party to me.

Indeed, the Republicans do have the worst sales pitch of the two major parties.

What is it? Basically, it is this: "We'll steal less of your money than the other guys."

While the Democrats promise a virtual utopia for the masses by taking money from the rich and giving it to the poor, the Republicans argue only over the percentage of taxpayer dollars that should be redistributed.

Republicans fail to challenge the legality, the constitutionality, and the morality of the system of "legalized theft" we have accepted in this country—a system that confiscates private property by brute force.

I just can't get excited about a party that accepts theft— even if it advocates cutting back the theft by 5 percent or 10 percent. Theft is wrong. It needs to be stopped. And precious few in either party are stating that obvious fact.

Some Republicans claim to oppose the federal income tax. Some even agree it is immoral and unconstitutional. But, they say, taking a hard-line stance against it won't achieve any results. It's not the politically savvy move. It takes time to undo a system that has been in place for ninety years.

I disagree. If something is morally wrong, you should oppose it categorically and not pull any punches. If it means election defeat, so be it.

Courageous leadership means saying and doing right no matter the results. Compromise with immorality and illegality is not a recipe for righteousness or success.

Other Republicans say they are simply afraid to take a strong stand against the Internal Revenue Service, for it has become akin to America's "Gestapo." There is a big price to pay for confronting the IRS, they explain. Even a member of Congress can and will be taken down—imprisoned, expelled, and disgraced—if he crosses the line and becomes too critical of the tax man.

To those Republicans, I say, "Get out of the way. If you are afraid to lead, if you are afraid to do what's right, what good are you?" Why do we need timid politicians who are going to pull punches when it comes to real evil within the government?

If we can't trust politicians to criticize the government, can we really trust them to make laws affecting our businesses, our property, our families, and our personal lives?

America is great because of founders who stood up and risked everything to fight tyranny. Today, we have politicians who are scared of their shadows. We have politicians interested only in featherbedding, in building their own power bases, and in securing their own futures and legacies.

You are getting ripped off. You are no longer a self-governing individual. You no longer live in a sovereign state. You no longer live in "a nation of the people, by the people, and for the people." Rather, it is a nation of the elite, by the elite, and for the elite.

And the Republican Party is a big part of the problem.

CHAPTER SIX

THIRD-PARTY ALTERNATIVES

T HE SERIOUS BUSINESS of building political parties does
not take place during presidential election years.

That's partly because the election game is rigged in favor
of the two major parties, which, after all, control the rules.
Democrats and Republicans may have nasty words for each
other in election years and off-election years, but one thing they
agree on is they like their duopoly of control over the process.

Democrats and Republicans write the campaign finance
regulations. Democrats and Republicans control the primary
process and the political conventions that get so much free
media attention and even federal government money! And,
speaking of media attention, think of how little focus is put on
what are perceived as minor parties that have no chance of
winning elections.

That deck is pretty stacked against the emergence of third
parties or third-party candidates or truly independent
candidates. The idea of achieving viability as a third party in a
presidential election year is somewhat of a stretch.

About the only factor that can change the dynamic slightly
is money. Remember Ross Perot's on-again, off-again campaign
for the presidency? He didn't come close to winning, but the
fortune he poured into his campaign almost surely had an
impact on the results in 1992.

And consider this: Theodore Roosevelt ran as a third-party candidate in 1912 and still got only 27 percent of the vote. Why is that important? Roosevelt was a former president and a beloved national figure. Yet even he couldn't buck the two-party system. No one else is likely to do it either.

No third-party candidate has a chance to win the electoral votes necessary to become president in 2008 unless the field becomes much more crowded.

Let's look at who else is running this year:

- Former Republican Rep. Bob Barr, the man who led the fight for impeachment of Bill Clinton, is heading the Libertarian Party ticket in 2008. Barr is a high-profile candidate for the party—a name known by far more people than Libertarian Party candidates of the recent past. He is a seasoned politician, smart and articulate. And, most of all, he is running in a presidential election year where there is great dissatisfaction about the choices. But Barr has some downsides, too. Though he claims to be a constitutionalist, upon being turned out of office, Barr joined the American Civil Liberties Union—anathema to many who would form his natural constituency.

- Chuck Baldwin won the nomination of the Constitution Party. He is running on a platform emphasizing national sovereignty and getting back to the Constitution, as his party's name implies. Baldwin is founder and pastor of the Crossroad Baptist Church in Pensacola, Florida, and hosts a weekly radio program called *Chuck Baldwin Live*. He has written two books—*Subjects Seldom Spoken On* and *This Is the Life*. He was the Constitution

Party vice presidential candidate in 2004. Baldwin is a true believer in the limited-government principles of the Constitution, but his strong isolationist and anti-war views will also somewhat limit his appeal to disaffected Republicans.

- Alan Keyes vied for the Constitution Party nomination and was defeated by the lesser-known Baldwin. He is now endorsed by America's Independent Party, but is unlikely to find his name on many state ballots because of the party's lack of funds and organization. Keyes is a former diplomat and three-time candidate for the Republican presidential nomination, as well as three-time candidate for the U.S. Senate, the most recent run being against Barack Obama in Illinois. But Keyes has never gotten much traction in any of his campaigns previously. Probably the most gifted orator in the race, Keyes has little financial support behind him and not much of an organization.

- Ralph Nader is another perennial candidate, but one who makes an impact because of his name recognition and appeal to the political fringe of the Democratic Party. The consumer advocate was a write-in candidate in 1992 and the Green Party nominee in 1996 and 2000. The significant percentage of the vote he received in 2000 may have prevented Al Gore from winning the presidency. This year he is running as an independent.

- The Green Party nominee, expected to be former Rep. Cynthia McKinney, will again siphon off some votes that might otherwise go to Barack Obama.

- The New American Independent Party, not to be confused with America's Independent Party, has nominated businessman Frank McEnulty.

- Jesse Johnson, a filmmaker and 2006 Senate candidate and 2004 gubernatorial candidate in West Virginia, has been nominated by the Green Party.

There will be other names on various ballots, and there is always the opportunity for any voter to write in the candidate or non-candidate of his or her choice.

Notably absent from the field of candidates is one who could have made a major impact, given his surprisingly strong showing in the Republican primary campaign. That is Ron Paul, who, instead of leaving the Republican Party, chose to run for re-election to his Texas congressional seat.

Since this was not the first presidential run for Ron Paul, I believe the support he got in his dark-horse bid for the Republican Party nomination is an indication of major disaffection from the policies of George W. Bush and the nominee in 2008, John McCain. While I had my own reasons for not supporting Paul in the primaries, I have great respect for those who did. For the most part, they are people who understand that our political system is severely broken, that America has been permitted to drift away from its constitutional moorings, and that it will take a radical change in direction to correct course.

There is no denying Ron Paul is a politician of consistency. He is a politician true to his beliefs and convictions. He is a politician who believes in the Constitution—honors it and reveres it. And that sets him apart from the front-running candidates of both parties.

Ron Paul showed America something in his 2008 race. Having observed his political career closely over thirty years, including his previous run for president, I never believed he could raise as much money as he raised, nor did I believe he could muster the popular support he mustered.

And he did it on principle, God bless him. Now, I have some fundamental disagreements with Ron Paul. They are so fundamental they prevented me from endorsing him. Yet he fared better in the primaries than the two men I chose—Tom Tancredo and Duncan Hunter.

Had Ron Paul decided to run as an independent candidate for president this year, I think he could have received 8 percent to 10 percent of the popular vote. He would have pulled votes most likely to go to McCain or Barr or Baldwin or even Nader. Because of his strong anti-war views, he may have even pulled a few votes from Obama.

But he's not in the race, and I will not pretend there is any other candidate running in 2008 who will, through the strength of his ideas, organization, and funding base, attract significant percentages of the vote. The Libertarian and Constitution Party candidates may indeed see record votes this year, but it will be largely a result of the weakness of the Republican ticket.

But my campaign for "none of the above" has nothing to do with winning the presidency for a third-party or independent candidate. That's not going to happen in 2008. The point of not voting for McCain or Obama transcends in importance who wins or loses the election this year.

It's about getting our own priorities straight. It's about sending a message. It's about ensuring that your vote is never again taken for granted. It's about making certain candidates address the real concerns of Americans. And, most important of all, it's about doing what's right.

Are we ready to give up on the Constitution?

Are we ready to give in to politicians who think they can do whatever they want regardless of the separation of powers and the restrictions on the federal government so clear in that document?

Are we ready to become just another nation in the world, forsaking our heritage of freedom and sovereignty?

It doesn't matter to me which of the independent or third-party candidates you support this year, or whether you support any of them. What is important is that you *not* support the business-as-usual Republican or Democratic candidates. It is important that you don't worry too much about the result. Either McCain or Obama is going to be the next president. In either case, America is in for a rough four years.

But that's all right. We should survive.

In fact, since 1960, we've had only eight good years of presidency.

Isn't that amazing?

We're losing our freedom in this country not because we elect bad presidents. We elect bad presidents because we're losing our freedom and our ability to discern right from wrong.

I'm not against trying to build a viable third party, but, as I said, it can't be done in the context of a presidential election year. It takes hard work years in advance of an election. We are probably many years away from seeing it happen in the United States.

Would I like to see one? Sure. I'd love to see America support several other parties. I'd love to see more competition and a broader political spectrum represented in our system. But, honestly, we don't absolutely *need* one.

What we need is an alternative to what has, in essence, become a one-party system in America today.

CHAPTER SEVEN

WHY A NEGATIVE VOTE IS A POSITIVE STEP

I T'S THE POLITICAL season, and many folks who normally hold high standards for leadership start getting weak in the knees. I know how this works. It happens to me, too. It happened to me, once again, in 2004—when I cast an admittedly defensive vote to avoid allowing John Kerry to become arguably the most powerful man in the world.

Many of us talk a great game when it comes to constitutional government, freedom, individual rights, national sovereignty, and self-government. It's easy to be principled in the abstract. Talk is cheap, as they say. Then elections roll around and we are usually faced with choices that don't move our nation any closer to these ideals.

Typically, we have a Democrat who believes in a "living Constitution" that means whatever the Supreme Court majority says it means—group rights, internationalism, and centralized power in Washington with virtually no limits. Then we have a Republican who believes in much of the same, that Congress and the president can pretty much do whatever they want, as if the Constitution didn't specifically restrict their powers to those enumerated by the founders.

How do we as voters respond?

One argument says we should hold out for principle, while the other suggests we all have to compromise and choose the lesser of two evils.

Let me suggest a good argument for holding out, sticking to principle, insisting on higher standards, boycotting elections where there is no clear choice, being very selective about the candidates for whom you support—and, sometimes, voting for "none of the above."

Let me explain this in market terminology.

If voters always choose the lesser of two evils, it is accurate to say they are not creating a market for excellence in politicians. They are creating a market for mediocrity in politicians.

Let's break it down to a smaller component. Each election, Republicans put up a candidate and Democrats put up a candidate. If 100 percent of Republicans vote for the Republican no matter his strengths or weaknesses, those party faithful are not encouraging the party leadership to find the best and the brightest, are they?

But if 5 percent hold out because a candidate is weak on, say, immigration issues, then the party leadership, if it's smart, will recognize what's happening and respond to the call of the marketplace.

That's the way marketplace politics could work, if it were tried, if it were practiced.

You don't even need third parties to make it work. Although they can help.

Some people claim you are "wasting your vote" if you sit out an election on principle. I would make the argument that voting for someone who is unfit to govern is the *real* waste of a vote.

Let's examine this concept further. Is it a waste of a dollar if you go to the store, don't see what you want, and decide not to spend it?

But if you spend that dollar just for the sake of spending it, are you likely to see better products—or even the specific one you really wanted? Do you find bargains by purchasing the first product you see while shopping? Are retailers likely to provide more choices to shoppers if shoppers are not discriminating? Of course not. They are going to provide fewer choices.

If customers walk into a shop and buy the first thing they see without regard to quality and price, what purpose would there be for retailers to provide more and better selections?

Let's say you are shopping for air conditioners for your house. The first unit you examine is not powerful enough to cool the house, has a track record of non-reliability, and is, in your opinion, excessively expensive. The second unit you look at has faulty wiring that may actually be dangerous to your home and family.

Do you buy the first model because it is the lesser of two evils? I don't think so. So why are Americans, who are generally savvy shoppers, so willing to accept the "lesser of two evils" principle when it comes to governing their country?

You might say: "Well, Farah, your shopping analogy doesn't hold up because, in politics, the whole nation has to choose one product in a presidential election. If we don't participate, the decision will be made for us."

No, the decision is being made for us now. For as long as Americans are of the mindset to vote for political product A or political product B, no matter how bad those choices might be, the choices in the future are likely to get increasingly worse.

In my book *Taking America Back*, in 2003, I challenged Americans to consider whether our national habit of voting for the lesser of two evils was always the best thing to do.

My thesis in a nutshell is this: never vote for any candidate who doesn't respect and revere and genuinely submit himself or herself to the authority of the U.S. Constitution and its strict limits on federal government power.

It sounds easy, but it's not.

There are precious few candidates for any office who fit that minimally acceptable description.

But why is that? It's because Americans no longer make it a requirement of their politicians.

It was not always this way.

There is much talk today about "judicial activism." Some Republicans decry when the Supreme Court exceeds its authority and legislates from the bench. The Supreme Court, they say, is supposed to interpret the Constitution, not expand it, not rewrite it, not amend it. I agree. However, we hear far fewer politicians decrying "legislative activism" or "executive activism." And few people have done more to expand "executive activism" than George W. Bush and Dick Cheney.

Just as the Constitution strictly limits the scope and authority of the Supreme Court, it also restricts the power of the Congress and the president. If you want to live in a free country governed by the rule of law and the will of the people, you have to hold politicians accountable not only to your will but to the Constitution that they swear an oath to uphold.

Every real American should be able to agree on this principle, but, unfortunately, those who really do, who take it seriously, who apply it to elections, represent a small minority.

What I am asking you to do in this book is to enlist in this budding movement. I am asking you to become one of the remnant of Americans who still get it, who understand why this country is different and better than any other in the world. I am asking you to think for yourself, not get herded like the rest of the sheep. I am asking you to make a stand for what's right.

I admit I yielded to the temptation to deviate from my own policy on one occasion—the 2004 presidential election. By then we knew George W. Bush had little understanding and respect for the Constitution, but, in a defensive strategy, to avoid the election of an outright traitor to his country in John Kerry, I wisely or unwisely decided to vote for Bush's re-election.

I'm still happy Kerry didn't win. But I take no little solace in whatever small part I played in Bush's undeserved re-election.

What can I say? I'm human. I'm a sinner. I live in a fallen world. I'm still not sure I would have acted any differently in 2004, knowing the imminent threat we faced from a Kerry presidency.

More than anything else, this choice illustrates again the political trap in which we find ourselves as a people. It's hard standing on principle. It's hard forsaking instant gratification for long-term good. It's hard not to choose the easy way—the way of delaying the day of reckoning.

But, I digress—back to the debate.

Some people obviously disagree with me—vociferously.

Richard Land, president of the Southern Baptist Convention's Ethics and Religious Liberty Commission, sounded off in a *Baptist Press* column about why we, as Christians, need to be willing to overlook the evil within candidates and actually have a moral obligation to make utilitarian compromises and vote only for those who are electable.[1]

The issue arose when James Dobson of Focus on the Family, Tony Perkins of the Family Research Council, and representatives of other Christian groups got together in Salt Lake City, pledging not to support a Republican nominee who was not "pro-life."

Here's part of what Land wrote: "Determining candidates' stances on moral issues should be a primary consideration; determining how the candidates' policy positions will benefit an individual personally (e.g., tax policies) should always be a secondary consideration."[2]

Notice what's missing? Any mention of the Constitution and the candidate's submission to it.

Also, Land makes a distinction between "moral issues" and tax policies. Let me explain that tax policy *is* a moral issue. It is immoral to steal. And when government uses force to take money from one person and give it to another, that's the moral equivalent of theft.

In fact, I would make the claim that every single thing the government does, everything in which it involves itself, every law and regulation and edict is an imposition of morality or immorality.

Moral issues are not just matters of life and death or sexuality. When Barack Obama, for example, makes plans to socialize healthcare in America, that is not only a bad idea, it is both immoral and unconstitutional.

Land says we should consult the Bible for the answers to questions we have about tough political choices. I agree. But I don't see anywhere in the Bible where it says we should embrace a little bit of evil to avoid a greater evil. I don't see anywhere in the Bible where it says we are to embrace a little bit of leaven. I don't see anywhere in the Bible where it suggests we should compromise with sin.

I'll tell you where this kind of thinking leads.

It leads to gutless choices. It leads to a slow death. It leads inexorably to loss of freedom. It's a kind of moral relativism—something Christians should avoid.

Our Founding Fathers recognized this. They had choices to make. Life under the crown of England wasn't intolerable. In fact, it was better than under most other tyrants in the world at the time. But they stood up for a better way. They risked everything for a chance to expand freedom. They were hardly the pragmatists Richard Land believes we need to be.

This type of compromise, this type of accommodation to the political zeitgeist, this type of moderation has led Richard Land astray in the past.

When Judge Roy Moore was taking a principled stand for the Constitution, God, country, faith, and family by defending the Ten Commandments monument in Alabama, where was Richard Land?

He was publicly challenging Moore, explaining that he disagreed with his tactics and strategy and equating the good judge's contest of a clearly unconstitutional federal order with "civil disobedience."

It sounds to me like Richard Land is more comfortable with the political status quo than standing up for truth, justice, and morality.

But there's more than just principle at stake in this election. I'm telling you to take a principled stand not just because I believe it is the right thing to do. I also truly believe it is the most *expedient* thing to do. Let me explain.

Only twice in my lifetime has America experienced the kind of clear political choice for president that I would like to see routinely, that I would expect to see routinely.

The first time that happened was when Ronald Reagan captured the Republican nomination for the presidency and faced incumbent Jimmy Carter. The second time was when Ronald Reagan ran as an incumbent president in 1984.

What was it that set us up for that memorable choice in 1980?

I'll tell you what it was. It was four years of hapless Jimmy Carter. In 1976, Americans were tired of political corruption and incompetence and took a chance on an unknown governor from Georgia. He seemed like a breath of fresh air. He seemed honest. (At least he kept telling us he was honest.) He promised "change" — without providing too much in the way of specifics.

He got the Democratic Party presidential nomination and challenged unelected president Gerald Ford, who had been appointed vice president by Richard Nixon before he resigned in disgrace. Carter went on to beat Ford.

But the change he promised was not the kind Americans had wanted. Jimmy Carter was a pushover for America's enemies. When the Soviets invaded Afghanistan, on a march they expected to make right into the Middle East, Carter's impotent response was to boycott the Olympics. When Iranian radicals took over the U.S. Embassy in Tehran, kidnapping U.S. personnel and holding them hostage for 444 days, Carter's response was his famous "Rose Garden strategy." He would not leave the White House until the enemy capitulated. Needless to say, the enemy never did during Carter's term of office. Instead they watched an ineptly planned rescue effort go up in flames and praised Allah for their good fortune. Compare this incompetence to what Ross Perot did. Perot successfully rescued two of his employees from an Iranian jail around the same time Carter's rescue helicopters crashed and burned.

Meanwhile, during those four years of Jimmy Carter's presidency, Americans, for the first time in history, began measuring their distress and suffering. This may seem like satire for those too young to remember those days, but the Carter administration prompted something called "the misery index," which measured Americans' woes and anxiety.

For his part, Carter blamed the American people for being in a "malaise." Of course, they were in a malaise. They had to wait for another election to be rid of the rascal who had fooled them into thinking he had real answers to America's problems.

I present this history to you to make a point. I believe the best way to get another choice like we had in 1980 is for Americans to have the opportunity, if you want to call it that, of seeing someone very much like Carter back in the White House and working with a House and Senate dominated by his own party.

I believe four years of Barack Obama will be terrible for America—in the short term. But they could prove to be very positive—in the long term. Why? For the same reason Jimmy Carter was terrible in the short term and positive in the long term.

Obama's policies of taxing and spending and clamping down on freedom in healthcare and other areas will prove massively unpopular when Americans see them fail, as they always do. Obama and the Democrats will try to blame past administrations for the problems, just as Jimmy Carter tried to do. They will try to blame the people, just as Jimmy Carter tried to do. But with Democrats running Congress and the White House, it will be easy for Americans to see who is to blame.

I can almost promise you Barack Obama will not be elected to a second term. He will, in all likelihood, just like Jimmy Carter, pave the way for a real Republican president in 2012—if indeed there is one in the wings.

On the other hand, let's pretend John McCain wins the presidency in 2008. In all likelihood, there will still be a Democrat-dominated Congress. While U.S. policies under McCain and a Democrat Congress will be nearly equally disastrous, it will be the Republican president who bears the brunt of the blame in 2012. Guess what we'll get then? We'll get Barack Obama anyway. Or, perhaps, Hillary Clinton.

In effect, by electing McCain, we are only delaying the inevitable day of reckoning. McCain won't change a thing. His election will only delay what almost certainly must come.

I don't know if there is a Ronald Reagan in the wings. I don't see him if he is there. But I hope you can see my point. If we are going to do better in the future, we must have higher standards for our politicians. Real standards can never be enforced when we routinely vote for the lesser of two evils.

Some will undoubtedly ask if I am suggesting a Barack Obama presidency will actually be better for America than a John McCain presidency. The shocking answer to that question is yes. I do believe America will be better off with Barack Obama in the White House for the next four years rather than John McCain. Please understand I am not advocating voting for him, as I made clear in previous chapters. But I point this out simply to illustrate that voting for what appears to be the lesser of two evils can actually be detrimental to the health of the country.

During the 1980 presidential debate, Reagan famously asked the American people, "Are you better off than you were four years ago?" They responded by choosing a new president. Simply put, the failures of Carter helped pave the way for the greatness of Reagan. Similarly, President Obama will be a bad president, and that might not be a bad thing for the country in the long term.

That's why I believe the best thing Americans can do when they go to the polls this November is to vote for "none of the above."

CHAPTER EIGHT

WHAT ABOUT CONGRESS?

THE BUDGET should be balanced. Public spending should be reduced. The arrogance of officialdom should be tempered, and assistance to foreign lands should be curtailed, lest Rome become bankrupt."[1] After making the prophetic proclamation above sometime around 45 B.C., Marcus Tullius Cicero, a Roman senator, was assassinated.

It's not always easy telling the hard truths.

It's not always safe.

It's not always profitable.

But tell them we must.

They say those who don't learn from history are doomed to repeat it. I believe the United States is slouching toward Rome—and a Cicero is nowhere to be found.

Where are we today compared to the empire that lasted five hundred years?

- National debt: $10 trillion.

- U.S. federal budget: over $3 trillion. That's 50 percent higher than it was in 2000.

- Trade deficit: $58 billion.

- No meaningful borders, with record immigration levels and no chance for assimilation.

- Total breakdown of education system.

- No common faith or unifying moral principles that bind the nation together.

- Even age-old institutions like marriage and parenthood are being redefined.

- In a time of relative peace, our military forces are stationed in more than one hundred foreign nations.

And now America finds itself in an election year in which there are plenty of Mark Antonys but no Ciceros—no wise old voices of reason, common sense, and good judgment.

The power of the state is on the rise, and the power of the people is on the decline.

We have our own versions of the Colosseum, albeit somewhat more humane. The American people are kept distracted by bread and circuses—NASCAR, the NFL, *American Idol*.

Votes are being purchased with foolish promises of free healthcare and nebulous pledges of "change" and "hope."

There isn't much to believe in anymore, so politicians invent new religions—like "global warming." If only we pay our tithes in "carbon credits," the gods of climate change will be merciful to us, we are assured. But if we do not reach deep into our pockets now and make sacrificial offerings, doom will be upon us all in the coming decades.

This was the nation that gave the world the concepts of self-government, removing the shackles from the people and placing them on the government, individual rights as unalienable gifts from God.

This was the nation that welcomed and rewarded personal achievement—recognizing that it was a blessing not just to the one honored, but to all.

Today the highest virtues are little more than meaningless, empty words—"tolerance," "diversity," "pluralism," "multi-culturalism."

There is no right and no wrong. Up is down, black is white, left is right.

Who would have believed the greatest and longest-lasting experiment in freedom and self-government would end like this?

Who would have believed a nation that raised up so many great minds of politics, science, business, and philosophy could be so easily led astray?

Who would have believed a nation built of sacrifice and honor would give up its birthright for a mess of pottage?

Neither a vote for Barack Obama nor a vote for John McCain is going to move the country in the direction of addressing any of these critical problems that face us. That's why I believe this is *the* year for voting "none of the above."

But that is my prescription for the presidential race. What about Congress? Should we, as some suggest, vote against all incumbents? Should we not vote for any Republicans or Democrats running for the House or Senate? Is it time to boycott all elections?

I believe the answer to all these questions is an emphatic no.

There are some good men and women running for Congress this year who need your support. They are as committed to taking the country back to its constitutional moorings as you and I are.

What we need to do in each race in the House and Senate is to apply the same standards we apply to the presidential race.

Is there a candidate who truly understands and supports the Constitution of the United States, not just in words but in actions?

If you find a candidate like that in your state or your district, support him or her with enthusiasm. Help that candidate's campaign with your time and energy. Support it with your financial contributions. And, most of all, don't forget to vote for that candidate and bring as many friends and relatives to the polls as you can.

We won't likely redeem either house of Congress in 2008, but it's important to have some voices of reason who will support the rule of law and the will of the people. If we're going to create a system of market-driven politics again in America, we need to start at all levels.

Ultimately, Congress is where the real power is—at least according to the Constitution. As important as it is for Congress to know what its real authority is vis-à-vis the constitutional balance of power, it is equally important we have senators and representatives who understand what Congress's authority is *not*.

Let's discuss some proposed actions that are *not* within Congress's authority:

- Imposing windfall profits taxes on oil companies
- Nationalizing oil companies
- Nationalizing the healthcare system
- Increasing federal funding of local schools
- Imposing more regulations on local schools
- Distributing massive new amounts of foreign aid to fight global poverty
- Trying to change the weather

These are just a few of the initiatives that will be on the table for Congress in 2009 no matter who becomes president of the United States. It is unlikely any of them can be stopped because of the political realities of this election year.

What are those political realities?

We are coming to the end of the second term of a president who is massively unpopular because of his conduct of the wars in Iraq and Afghanistan as well as his handling of illegal immigration and the border. There are other reasons for his unpopularity, but, I believe, they would be inconsequential to George W. Bush's legacy had he unleashed our military forces to, without concern for our image throughout the world, achieve quick and decisive victory in Iraq and Afghanistan and secured the United States–Mexico border while enforcing immigration laws within the country.

But Bush didn't do those things. For too long he and Defense Secretary Don Rumsfeld pursued a "light footprint" strategy that dragged the war out unnecessarily.[2] Only with the surge strategy have we seen real progress in Iraq.

And not only will his legacy suffer as a result, but so will the Republican Party.

John McCain may win the presidency. But, if he does, it will be because of the extreme weakness of his Democratic opponent, not a tribute to his own popularity. In Congress, there is almost no chance for Republicans to make gains. It is in the House and Senate where Bush will cost his party.

Democrats will almost assuredly win even more seats in the Congress than they already control decisively. That's why all of the unconstitutional initiatives above will not only be introduced in 2009, they will receive broad support. In fact, they will receive, in many cases, bipartisan support.

America could be fundamentally changed as a result—and it won't make much difference which candidate wins the presidency. To one extent or another, both McCain and Obama believe the federal government can do whatever it wants despite the strict limits the Constitution imposes on its powers.

We can prepare for massive new tax increases. Even the modest income tax relief pushed through Congress by Bush will be repealed. Obama has made it clear he opposes it. Indeed, Obama has promised to raise the capital gains tax that Bill Clinton reduced. And McCain? He opposed the Bush tax cuts even as a sitting Republican senator!

Imagine that! America is in a recession or close to one. Normally this is the time government considers economic stimulus measures that mean putting more of people's money back in their pockets. But that's not where we're likely to go in 2009.

Constitutionally and morally, we should be supporting candidates who want to end the income tax. There are so many reasons to hate the frustrating and idiotic income tax, but let me focus on just one today.

Imagine you want to buy a new car. You find the make and model you like. You're pretty certain about the color and the options. You take your choice for a test drive.

Then you get down to haggling over the price.

"Now what about the price?" you ask the salesman.

"Depends," he says. "How much money do you earn?"

"Why is that any of your business?" you respond.

"Because," he says, "the price of the car depends on your salary."

"Why?" you ask incredulously.

"Oh, yeah," he explains. "If you make a hundred thousand dollars or more, you pay fifty percent more than someone who earns only, say, fifty thousand dollars. We're now selling cars the progressive way. We use a graduated cost index—or GCI—to figure out what our customers pay."

I'm sure if this happened to you, you'd be pretty steamed. Imagine if the cost of goods was determined by a sliding scale based on what we earned. It would be unbelievable, unthinkable, un-American.

Yet, why is it that we as Americans sit idly by while the federal government uses just such an unfair system of sliding scales to determine what our individual burdens are?

Isn't that just what the so-called progressive tax system is all about? Isn't that what the graduated income tax is?

In fact, the government's scam is even worse than my hypothetical. We each pay taxes to the federal government according to what we earn. But we don't necessarily get anything more in return when we pay more. In fact, generally speaking, those who pay nothing or less get more under the Infernal Revenue Disservice plan.

Until we dismantle—once and for all—the criminal tax code, more of this fraud and thievery will find its way into American life.

Why do we accept such a system as rational?

Why do we accept this as just?

Why do we accept this as legal?

Doesn't such a system clearly diminish our hard work? Doesn't it provide disincentives to make more money, to put capital at risk, and to provide jobs for others? How is any of that beneficial to society?

In other words, we accept irrational actions from the supposedly accountable government that we would never accept from private industry.

In fact, I'm sure there are laws against charging customers different prices for the same product. Only government could get away with this. Only the government believes it has the right and the duty to charge us different amounts for goods and services we may or may not want, and to use force if necessary to extract those funds from us.

Come on! This is not the Soviet Union. It's the United States of America.

It's time for a change. It's time to de-Sovietize America!

If you find candidates for Congress this year who understand this principle, get behind them.

Likewise, if you find candidates for Congress this year who understand why America needs to remain sovereign and independent—the way our forefathers intended—get behind them.

We all know America was founded on the idea of independence. We fought a war of independence to secure our freedom from, at the time, the most powerful empire in the world. But that was then. This is now.

Today, we're moving perilously close to giving it all up. We're told we live in an "interdependent" world and that this is a good thing. But "interdependent" is just a synonym for "dependent." How? One way is through so-called free trade agreements.

I've always been sort of agnostic when it comes to "free trade."

On the one hand, I could see the economic benefits of truly "free" trade.

Yet, on the other hand, I could definitely see some real problems with what is often mistakenly referred to as "free trade" in the world today.

For instance, there's nothing "free" about the North American Free Trade Agreement. I certainly have not witnessed any benefits to the people of the United States in the fifteen years it has been around. And, I strongly suspect, Mexicans, who have fled to the United States in one of the greatest refugee exoduses in the history of the world, don't think it has helped their native country.

Real free trade is pretty simple, really. When two countries remove tariffs by mutual agreement, you have free trade. That's not what NAFTA's about. Nor is the World Trade Organization about real free trade. I doubt there is a single human being alive who has read the thousands of pages of arcane rules and regulations making up each of these monstrosities and dozens of other trade agreements signed.

I have come to believe some of the greatest economic minds of our time have been snookered by the redefinition of "free trade." For years I have wanted to believe what mentors like Walter Williams, who is generally right about everything, have written and said—that the alarmingly high trade deficit facing the United States today is really not threatening at all. Some even argue it is a good thing.

For those of you struggling like I did with the meaning of the increasingly staggering U.S. trade deficit—now approaching $60 billion—I have news for you: this trade deficit is *not* a good thing.

In fact, I would argue the trade deficit could cripple the U.S. economy, bankrupt the U.S. government, and destroy our freedom.

The U.S. trade deficit is the result of foreign government currency manipulations and suicidal subsidies the U.S. tax system gives to foreign savings. And it is destroying the manufacturing base in the United States that is critical to American security.

They say there's nothing new under the sun—and I agree. "Free trade," though, is often billed as something new. All one really needs to do to see what happens to an empire that relies on foreign manufacturers is to ask yourself why Spain no longer rules the world.

In the sixteenth century, Spain was the world's powerhouse. The age of discovery was kind to Spain. The Spanish crown had colonized the New World and plundered its gold to finance its rise on the world stage. When Spain needed something, it could buy it from France or England, which didn't have nearly as much gold but were developing manufacturing bases.

According to the conventional "free trade" theories, this kind of exchange should have been healthy for all three economies. Yet, while France and England prospered, Spain's reliance on foreign manufacturing signaled its death knell as a preeminent world power.

America today is the Spain of the sixteenth century—forsaking its manufacturing base for the privilege of buying cheap goods from foreign manufacturers. The United States pays not with gold, but with dollars that are increasingly losing their value and trade debt that can never be repaid.

Now those foreign manufacturers, mainly government-controlled companies in China, are lending money to Americans so they can keep buying their inferior, albeit cheap, goods. American manufacturers, beset by minimum-wage laws, safety regulations, environmental rules, workmen's compensation claims, unions, taxes and a thousand other obstacles not faced by China Inc., can't even begin to compete.

We may not have been able to see the extent of the damage to our infrastructure ten years ago. But it is more than evident today. The chickens have, indeed, come home to roost.

How bad can it get?

The trade deficit is not sustainable. It will eventually lead to the collapse of the dollar, depression, and conversion of the United States to a second-rate power.

John McCain isn't going to reverse this course. Neither is Barack Obama. That's why we need a few brave and courageous and independent voices in the U.S. Congress more than ever. Find them. Elect them. Don't just stay home in November because of the poor choices at the top of the ticket. Understand you can still make a difference in other important races and on critical ballot measures at the local and state levels.

Things will get worse in the next four years—no matter how we vote. For example, let's just look at one issue. There is no will among either McCain or Obama or the Congress of the United States to secure the border and address rampant illegal immigration.

We are now at the point as a nation where Americans are going to be feeling the economic pinch from the uncontrolled immigration of the last two decades. George Bush is wrong when he says the illegal immigrants are just doing the jobs Americans don't want to do. In fact, they are doing many of the jobs Americans would like to do—but they are doing them cheaper, pricing honest, hard-working, law-abiding U.S. citizens out of the job market in many, many cases.

I've been saying for years that young Americans just don't have the opportunities for a first job we once had in this country—due to a combination of illegal immigration and government rules and regulations that discourage the hiring of kids.

And this is just one of dozens of reasons to oppose illegal immigration.

Here are some others we should not forget:

- Crime.

- Traffic.

- Driving safety.

- National security.

- Drugs.

- Diseases.

- National sovereignty.

- Amnesty doesn't work.

- Assimilation of vast numbers of immigrants takes too long.

- It attacks what holds us together—common language and culture.

- It creates resentment among the new underclass.

- It is an immoral infringement on the right of all citizens who are forced to accept national IDs, cameras, and other intrusive forms of surveillance in a once-free society.

- It victimizes foreigners who play by the rules.

- It is an affront to the rule of law.

- It is a drain on America's healthcare system.

- It drives up taxes.

- It reduces wages for American workers in the lower rungs of the economic ladder.

- It takes the lives of many migrants.

- When husbands and fathers emigrate for work, it splits families apart.

Because of illegal immigration and a border that remains insecure, life in America will become noticeably less pleasant in the next four years:

- Fewer jobs, more competition for them

- Higher taxes, fewer services

- More privileges for special interest groups, less equality under the law

- More government intervention, less freedom

- More violations of the Constitution, less rule of law

Today's politicians talk about change and promise Americans their wildest dreams are going to come true if only they are elected. But the day of reckoning is coming. These politicians will soon be out of excuses. I would say that day of reckoning is only four years away.

In this political season, it is important to remember the Democrats have controlled Congress for forty-one of the last fifty-three years. During that same time, they controlled the White House twenty-six of fifty-three years.

Yet they never seem to accomplish what they promise their constituents—the elimination of poverty and homelessness, a more humane and just society, and peace with our neighbors around the world.

If Barack Obama is the president for the next four years, and he has the backing of a Democratic Congress, how are the Democrats going to explain the disaster they create with their wrongheaded ideas? I say, let them do it. It will be a service to the country in the long run if everyone can see just how rotten these failed ideas are. Go for it! Let's give them four years, as we did from 1976 to 1980. Apparently many Americans have forgotten what the Carter years were like. Many Americans are too young to have experienced them. Maybe we have to again live that kind of malaise, that kind of depression, that kind of defeat to learn from it.

CHAPTER NINE

WHY CONSERVATISM IS NOT ENOUGH

I*S THE PROBLEM* with the two leading candidates for president in 2008 that they are not conservative enough?
No.

That is not the problem.

The problem is that the conservative agenda is not enough to reclaim America's freedom. The problem is that "conservative" doesn't mean anything anymore. The problem is that we need a more radical prescription for turning the country around, not a more tepid one, not a more defensive one, not a more conservative one.

In this world of left versus right, of liberal versus conservative, of Democrat versus Republican, you may never have heard such a message before. It may seem like I'm parsing words, nitpicking, trying to rewrite the modern political lexicon.

But this distinction is important, because there are some fundamental problems with the term "conservative."

You might recall the aftermath of the 2006 midterm election. The conservative mantra about the Republican drubbing in the midterm congressional elections is: "Conservatives didn't lose; Republicans did."

With all due respect to my conservative friends, this is the kind of thinking that will take them the way of the Whigs.

Don't get me wrong. I love conservatives. Some of my best friends label themselves as such. But think seriously about this: Being "conservative" is not a bold vision for the future. Being "conservative" will never inspire Americans to reject socialism and immorality. Being conservative will never bring back constitutionally limited government.

Banking on this vague and increasingly meaningless descriptive, this wholly inadequate, timid ideology is, instead, a surefire recipe for political defeat for the foreseeable future.

Conservatives were both right and wrong in their critique of Republicanism in 2006.

It's true that Republicans did not distinguish themselves from their Democratic counterparts. It's true that Republicans did nothing to hold on to their political base. It's true that Republicans governed just like Democrats.

But, I have to tell you, "conservatism" is not the recipe for taking America back. It won't work.

There are three fundamental problems with conservatism:

- It is a defensive movement rather than offensive.

- Its exclusive field of battle is electoral politics.

- It lacks the vision of a better future.

America is sliding inevitably toward socialism and immorality. I'm not going to call the direction we're moving "liberalism," because that description is simply too kind and understates the seriousness of our crisis and the lateness of the hour.

Forget about who won Congress. Look at the way Americans voted on issues.

While it's true that marriage amendments passed in all but one state—Arizona—the closeness of all those tallies is what disturbs me. It persuades me the conservative agenda is an agenda that just keeps losing ground.

You would think that amendments simply declaring marriage to be an institution between one man and one woman would garner at least 90 percent support among Americans.

Yet, even in four states in which the amendment passed, opposition exceeded an astounding 40 percent of the vote!

Conservatives look at those numbers and see victory. I've got news for you: so do the same-sex marriage activists. I look at those numbers and see inevitable defeat. It might be in 2008 or 2010 or 2012. But the die is cast. There is no question the American view of marriage is changing.

Why is it changing? Because the people no longer have a vision. As the Bible states, "Where there is no vision, the people perish: but he that keepeth the law, happy is he."[1]

America needs a vision again. It needs a return to morality—an understanding and appreciation of right and wrong. And it needs a return to the rule of law.

The conservative agenda is not sufficient for that purpose— not even close.

The defensive agenda of conservatives is failing—and it will continue to fail. And the way society views marriage today is just one example of hundreds in the way it is failing.

It's time for conservatives to realize the problem is not limited to the Republican Party. There is something inherently inadequate with the conservative vision.

Let me put it to you this way: after Nancy Pelosi and Harry Reid and Charles Rangel and John Conyers and Barack Obama or John McCain have their way with America, will you, as a conservative, be satisfied with preserving or conserving what's left of America?

I'm not content with that prospect even right now—before they take the country further down their slippery slope of moral relativism and tyranny.

At some point, and I believe we're long past that point, "conserving" the vestiges of American institutions will no longer be adequate. I think we've already lost way too much freedom and morality. We need a counterrevolution to restore them—not an effort to save what's left.

Let me illustrate what is happening this way: Imagine American politics as a tug-of-war. One side in the battle is actually playing to win—to pull its opponents into the moat. The other side, though, is simply trying not to get pulled into the moat.

Who is inevitably going to win? Which political ideology do you think is represented by the team whose goal is a standoff?

I know this is hard to understand because no one else— and I mean *no one*—is saying what I am saying.

Like it or not, the very nature of the word "conservative" defines the ideology. It is not a radical movement to expand freedom and economic opportunity. It is not a radical movement to restore justice and morality. It is not a radical movement to achieve victory over evil.

Instead, it is a "conservative," defensive movement that is merely content standing still. Most scholars trace conservatism's founding back to Edmund Burke, a British statesman in the eighteenth century. Essentially, Burke's theory was that conservatives should practice evolution instead of revolution, or moderate change instead of drastic change.[2] And that's why conservatism isn't enough.

What America needs today is a radical movement.

Unfortunately, in the history of the world, there is no such thing as a social movement that stands still. You are either moving toward your goal or moving away from it.

What are the conservatives' goals? Let's say "preserving marriage" is one of them. The way conservatives fight to achieve their status quo goal is to get marriage amendments on ballots. At first they win one referendum after another. Conservatives see victory at hand—even though, if they are 100 percent successful, all their hard work and sacrifice will have gone to the goal of achieving the status quo.

Meanwhile, the other side doesn't worry too much about those votes. Instead, they are fighting in a whole different arena—the battle for the hearts and minds of the American people using the cultural institutions of the press, the entertainment industry, the foundations, the corporations, the elite universities, and even the churches.

That's why each successive vote on marriage amendments is a little closer. Their goal is the destruction of the very building block of Western civilization—the traditional family.

The American people have been softened up and are starting to believe that marriage between same-sex couples is perfectly normal and acceptable—a notion that would have been anathema to them twenty years ago.

This is an illustration of the inadequacy of the conservative agenda.

It's hard to accept for conservatives who have placed so much faith in this ideology of defeat.

"Are you saying, Farah, that conservatism can never triumph?" you might ask. "What about Ronald Reagan?"

It's a good question. Conservatism does have its momentary political triumphs. They can occur when life under socialism and immorality becomes intolerable for people. If conservatism is packaged well and articulated by an articulate and passionate personality, it can win at the polls—no question about it.

Yet the cultural march toward socialism and immorality continues unabated—just as it did during the Reagan years.

Personally, I have come to detest the label "conservative."

I've said it before and I guess I have to say it again: I am not a conservative.

Nothing bothers me quite so much as when I am labeled one—or, worse yet, when my news agency, WorldNetDaily, is labeled "conservative." It's difficult for me to understand how my creation could be so simplistically and erroneously mislabeled as "conservative."

In fact, why does our entire national debate have to be reduced to terms such as "liberal," "moderate," and "conservative"?

Now, don't take offense if you proudly consider yourself a "conservative," "moderate" or "liberal." As I said, some of my best friends do. But I don't. In fact, I am offended when labeled like this. I'm offended when the fruits of my hard labors are reduced to bumper-sticker slogans. And I think it is important to raise the level of the national dialogue.

We have come to view politics in America through this prism of right versus left, conservative versus liberal, Republican versus Democrat—as if that's all there ever was, as if that's all there is, as if that's all there ever will be. It's not true.

In his famous 1964 television address on behalf of Barry Goldwater, Ronald Reagan said that there is no left or right, only up or down.[3] He was right. Sadly, we still insist on defining ourselves with "left" and "right"", liberal" and "conservative."

These terms are misleading. They mean different things to different people at different times. When I hear hard-line totalitarians in China referred to as "conservatives," I know I never want to be confused with them. When I hear George W. Bush call himself a "compassionate conservative," I know I never want to be confused with his political philosophy. When I hear the Nazis described as "right-wingers," I know I never want to be confused with them.

Frankly, if these labels represented the totality of the political spectrum, it would represent no choice at all—and that is precisely what we have with the major-party presidential nominees in 2008.

Let me get personal again for a minute. I've been a newsman my whole adult life. This is what I do. Yes, I have strong personal opinions that I share freely and openly on a daily basis. I write books. I publish them. But my main occupation has been, is, and always will be "newsman."

I believe the proper role of a newsman is to seek the truth without fear or favor. Unlike many of my colleagues in the press, I have avoided political parties, organizations, and associations that could compromise my integrity.

My worldview undoubtedly shapes the way I see the world, just as the worldviews of all other newsmen shape their perceptions. But my worldview is hardly "conservative."

By definition, conservatives seek to "conserve" the best of the status quo. In other words, they constantly are on the defense— busy holding on to turf, rather than taking new ground.

That strikes me as a recipe for failure, defeat, retreat, compromise. I don't believe we live in a time for defensiveness—not for people who want to seek truth, spread justice, and expand freedom.

I'm not a "conservative" because I see precious little left in this world worth conserving. Playing defense, it seems to me, can only forestall an inevitable slide into tyranny. If we're not seeking truth, spreading justice, and expanding freedom, we are losing ground. There are no holding actions—not for long. My goal is to restore the dream that was America.

And that dream was, is, and always will be radical.

Was George Washington a "conservative"? No. He was a revolutionary. He was known throughout the world as "the father of freedom."

Today, those who stand for truth, justice, freedom, the rule of law, self-government, and the moral principles of the Bible are not part of "the establishment." We're the rebels, the radicals, the revolutionaries. By the world's standards, we're the renegades.

I want Americans thinking outside the box. I want Americans setting their standards high. I want Americans remembering what made this country great. I want Americans embracing their Creator-God and living for Him. I want to cultivate a new generation of truth seekers, justice spreaders, and freedom expanders.

Let me be blunt about this "conservative" issue: the conservative movement is dead.

It has, as Rush Limbaugh would say, assumed room temperature. It is deceased. It has checked out. It has departed this earthly plane. It is gone, over, completed, finished.

It died young. It began in earnest with the failed Barry Goldwater presidential bid in 1964. It reached its pinnacle of power and influence during Ronald Reagan's presidency from 1981 through 1989 and was resurrected briefly in 1994 when Republicans, led by Newt Gingrich, took over both houses of Congress. Very briefly.

It was euthanized by President George W. Bush.

That is the short, bittersweet history of the modern conservative movement—one that championed so much of what is right, but did so with tactics and strategies that were so wrong.

As I pointed out earlier in this chapter, no political movement, relying on popular support, can ever succeed without the following:

- A definition of success

- An offensive agenda for achieving that success

- A long-term battle plan for cultural renewal, not just short-term political victories

On the first score, conservatives have not been successful at painting a picture of what they want America to look like in the future. They can tell you they want less government. They can tell you they believe in personal responsibility. They can tell you they believe in free enterprise.

But, on the details, it gets a little murky. There's little consensus among those who define themselves as conservatives about how much less government they want, how much they are willing to rely on personal responsibility in a world stricken with moral rot, and when free enterprise simply becomes avaricious multinational corporatism.

The most serious deficiency in conservatism is that it offers no "offensive" agenda. It is a well-meaning ideology that fights exclusively on the defense.

Except in football, you cannot win with defense alone.

You can't win a battle with defense alone. You can't win a war with defense alone. And you cannot win a political struggle with defense alone. The very term "conservative" strongly connotes the defensive nature of the movement. It is about "conserving" rather than advancing. It is about holding on to turf rather than taking new ground.

Conservatives too often define themselves by what they are against rather than what they are for. It's understandable in a world literally dominated by socialism, moral relativism, and tyranny.

Further, conservatism is a movement almost exclusively limited to the battleground of politics—specifically electoral politics.

Those whom conservatives oppose don't have to win elections to achieve their goals. They press their agendas through the culture. They use the press, the entertainment industry, the major foundations, government-sponsored media, the education system, academia, and so on, to change the way people think. When that fails, they use government agencies, including the courts, to force their will on the people.

With rare exceptions, conservatives don't engage the major cultural institutions. They criticize them. But they do little to take them over and use them to their advantage.

I understand it is difficult to discard convenient, self-assuring labels in what appears to be a world of dualistic choices—liberal and conservative, Democrat and Republican, Tweedle-dee and Tweedle-dum.

But if you doubt what I am saying, consider this year's presidential election choices.

One of the ways George W. Bush euthanized the conservative movement was through his use of the term "compassionate conservative."

The minute I heard that, I knew what was up—and I wrote about it, warned about it. First of all, as should be clear by now, I hate labels—especially political labels. Usually they are meant to deceive rather than enlighten the public. We don't have to look back too far into the past to remember that Bill Clinton wasn't just a "Democrat." He described himself as a "New Democrat." Of course, there was really nothing "new" about him. The adjective was simply an attempt to shake off the baggage his party had accumulated in the previous thirty to forty years. He was going to be different, he promised. Perhaps the only real difference with Clinton turned out to be the fact that he was a master manipulator, a political chameleon who often succeeded in his attempts to be all things to all people. But the label was more style than substance—as most labels are.

Then came George W. Bush, the "compassionate conservative," vying for the throne. It was another bait-and-switch routine. He was pulling a Clinton.

Conservatives did have lots of baggage they would like to discard. For many Americans, the perception was that conservatives were mean. They were just trying to cut all those benefits for poor people, for children, for the underprivileged. For others, the perception was that conservatives were ill equipped to govern, to roll back the advances of socialism in any meaningful way.

The results of the failed "Republican Revolution" of 1994 did little to change that image. Few Americans were satisfied with the results.

So along came George W. Bush and his "compassionate conservatism."

The clear insinuation of the term was that conservatism— the philosophy that theoretically emphasizes less government— must be tempered with compassion to make it more humane.

Should we expect any more from a nation of enablers and co-dependents? That's what America has become. And government is the enabler-in-chief. "Compassionate conservatism," as I explained before George W. Bush ever took office, would mean "socialism lite."

Is there anything compassionate about sustaining people in their pathologies? Of course not. How many people do you know who make wrong-headed choices with their life based on "compassion"? It's the same with government politics based on misguided compassion.

A perfect example is the minimum wage. Everyone in Washington—Democrats and Republicans alike—seems to agree that we should raise the minimum wage as an act of compassion for the poor. The truth is that there are few policies I can think of that are less compassionate toward the poor.

If you really want to help the poor, eliminate the minimum wage. You would see an explosion of new jobs and opportunities for young people to get their foot in the door of the workplace for the first time. It would be such a shot in the arm to the economy. The people who would benefit most would be those who are struggling. Instead, the government attempts artificially to inflate paychecks through mandate. The result, of course, is fewer jobs, less opportunity.

Is there anything compassionate about that result?

No, but those who speak of compassion in politics don't measure results. They measure feelings, poll results, intentions.

I don't think America will listen, but the prescription for what ails this country is not more phony compassion and certainly not more lip service to conservatism. What it needs is a dose of reality. It's as if America has been walking around in a drug-induced stupor in recent years. Maybe it's television. Maybe it's the hallucinogenic effect of the popular culture. Maybe it's the frontal lobotomy known as public education our kids are enduring.

The most successful politicians recognize the state of the nation and play to it. You want a nanny? The politician will be your nanny. You want a daddy? The politician will be your daddy. You want a big brother? The politician will be only too happy to be Big Brother.

America—you don't need or want *any* of those things. Instead, you need to get off your fat, pampered butts and take care of yourselves. You need to reject government "help" altogether. Stop turning from tweedle-dee to tweedle-dum and expect anything to change. No presidential candidate is going to save you.

Govern thyself.

What do we do differently?

One of the leading conservative think tanks in Washington has been running a media campaign this year called "What Would Reagan Do?"

No, don't get me wrong, I love and admire Ronald Reagan and what he did for this country as much as anyone. But he was hardly infallible. He was hardly perfect. In fact, as much as I like Reagan, there is something a little offensive about that slogan, given its obvious origin. It was Charles Sheldon in his great book *In His Steps* who popularized the question "What would Jesus do?" It took on new life with a merchandising blitz a decade or so ago.

For Christians to ask the question "What would Jesus do?" is entirely appropriate, given our belief that He is the Son of God, the everlasting Prince of Peace, the Savior, the future King. Substituting any mortal's name into that question, though, is a mistake.

We should not guide our behavior or our politics by the standards of one man—not even one great man.

We can certainly learn from great men of the past—including Reagan. But I would propose we look even further back—to more imperfect men, those who gave us this unique experiment in freedom.

I'm talking, of course, about the Founding Fathers. These were truly great men, whose work and dedication and insight and sacrifice can and should be appreciated more today than ever before.

As I alluded to earlier, George Washington was no conservative. Neither was Thomas Jefferson or James Madison or John Adams. They were all imperfect men, as they would be the first to admit. But they shared a vision for a great, free, moral nation—one that could both learn from the mistakes of the past and be inspired by the wisdom of the ages.

Their plan was simple yet truly revolutionary in the history of the world. It was to take the shackles off the people and place them on the government.

They understood the threat to freedom always comes from government. They also recognized people living in a fallen world needed order—the kind of order that can come only with a limited amount of central government. They believed the best form of government was one scarcely understood today—self-government.

They also understood only a moral people who truly believed they were accountable to God were capable of self-government.

America has much work to do in setting itself on a course correction that will result in expanding freedom, restoring justice, and increasing morality. It will not happen overnight. It will not happen as a result of electoral politics alone. It will not happen because we wish it to happen.

It will happen only if those of us who get it, who appreciate the contributions and sacrifices our founders made in giving us independence and a Constitution to guide us, and who recognize they are accountable to the sovereign God of the universe start taking real action—the kind of bold, courageous, and inspired action our forefathers took.

I believe the purpose of this book, to persuade you to break from the mindless business-as-usual politics of the past, is in line with that mission.

Let's start today.

Let's redefine ourselves as freedom fighters, rather than Democrats or Republicans or conservatives or liberals.

Let's insist that the governing standard of America be the Constitution.

Let's send a message in 2008 that will be heard around the world.

CHAPTER TEN

WHY POLITICS IS NOT ENOUGH

D OES ANYONE BELIEVE that if Americans elected the right
person as president that we would really be on our way
to addressing the nation's fundamental problems?

Does anyone believe that if Americans filled Congress with
the best available candidates *and* elected a righteous president
that the country would be out of danger from further decay?

The sad truth is that America's most pressing problems are
well beyond the scope and ability of our political class to solve.

Why is that? Well, let's take a look at what some of those
problems are:

- The breakdown of the institutions of
  marriage and family

- The inability for many to distinguish between
  right and wrong

- The consolidation of power in Washington
  and in the executive branch

- The breakdown in the rule of law

- The usurpation of power by unaccountable
  supra-national agencies

- Infringements on personal freedoms

- Increasing vulnerability to weapons of mass destruction

What do these and other problems our nation is facing have in common?

While government has contributed to their creation and fueled these crises, they all have spiritual and cultural dimensions, too. They have something else in common, as well. They were not created overnight and they will not be fixed overnight. The problems we're facing in America today—and, in fact, the problems faced by others around the world—did not occur by accident or by chance. They are actually the result of real planning, real plotting, and real scheming.

Back in the early 1900s, an Italian Communist by the name of Antonio Gramsci came up with an idea for achieving the goals of socialism without firing a shot. He suggested that fellow travelers should embark on a long march through the cultural institutions—subverting, changing their missions, taking them over. He believed that if socialist ideas permeated the most influential non-political aspects of society—education, the philanthropies, the entertainment industry, the press—that political power would literally fall into the laps of those who chose such a path.

Gramsci, whose work has been translated into dozens of languages, wrote that the most important task in this long-term plan for winning the hearts and minds of the people was to attack the notion that there is a sovereign God who endows His creatures with certain inalienable rights and who establishes absolute rules about right and wrong.

Can anyone doubt that the current state of the world is very much the legacy of Gramsci and others who shared his ideas? Can anyone doubt that the culture is the Ho Chi Minh trail to political power?

But, to be honest, the world's problems cannot be totally laid at the feet of Gramsci and his socialist disciples. There's much more at work here—darker forces, invisible forces, sinister forces, diabolical forces. What we're seeing in America today is real-world evidence of the spiritual warfare described in the Bible—the unseen powers and principalities referred to by Paul in Ephesians 6:12. The world is a battleground in a universal struggle between the forces of good and the forces of evil.

For those of us who understand Paul, believe what he wrote, and believe in the God whom He served, there is reason for great optimism. We know how all this is going to work out. We've read the end of the book.

Jesus is going to come back and straighten out this mess. For those who know Him and don't live to see that day, they will live with Him for eternity in paradise. You can't get a much better ending than that.

I can certainly understand why those who don't believe are gloomy as they look out at the deterioration of the world around them. I can understand why they are desperate to find a political messiah. I can understand why they want a quick fix on Election Day. But why are those of us who do believe so pessimistic?

We, too, are gloomy because we want to do something now. We want to right injustice. We want to protect our kids from harm. We know we have a responsibility to do something, and it's frustrating as we watch the world fall apart around us.

I do believe conditions are going to worsen before they get better. Not all Christians agree. I think America is headed for much tougher times—perhaps as a judgment for so much sin and immorality amid such blessings.

How do we fight back in the spiritual realm? As the Bible tells us, we put on the "whole armor of God" (Ephesians 6:11, 6:13). We do that by immersing ourselves in His word. We pray unceasingly. We ask God's blessing and mercy on us.

In other words, we wage spiritual warfare by practicing combat faith. Combat is not a nine-to-five job. It's not a hobby. It's a way of life, a mindset, an attitude. To do it effectively, you have to be tough and serious about it. It requires training and discipline.

But the good news is that we have already won the war. The outcome is assured. All we must do is endure, accept our responsibilities, do our duty, be good soldiers.

Just as spiritual war requires spiritual combat, cultural war requires cultural combat.

It's our duty then, those of us who believe in God and the freedom and responsibility He represents, to begin a process of what I call "reverse Gramsciism." It's time to begin another long march through the cultural institutions.

It's not a time for timidity or compromise. It's not a time for defensiveness and conciliation. It's time to take the offensive in this struggle.

As you learned in the last chapter, I'm not a "conservative." I'm not a conservative because I see precious little left in this world worth conserving. Conservatives will never make good cultural warriors because they are always on the defensive—trying to conserve or preserve something.

But when an apple turns rotten, there's no sense in trying to preserve it. You just throw it out.

Was Jesus a conservative? No, he was not. He was a radical. He was a revolutionary. He came to Earth to overthrow the world order—and He did. For those of us who follow Him, that remains our mission today. And we better realize it.

Were the Apostles Peter and Paul conservatives? No, they were not. They turned the world upside down, as contemporary historians noted.

Was George Washington a conservative? No. He was a revolutionary who practiced combat faith.

Today, those who stand for freedom, justice, the rule of law, and the principles of the Bible are not part of "the establishment." We're the rebels. By the world's standards, we're the renegades. We need to be proud of that and stop trying to preserve a rotten apple.

What is the rotten apple? You can see it in the government schools that dumb down American kids. You can see it in the universities that pervert the concepts of knowledge and wisdom, in the federalization and militarization of law enforcement, in the proliferation of non-constitutional government, in the real "trickle-down economics" of confiscatory taxes, in the unaccountable authorities that give us global treaties, in the relentless attacks on marriage and the family, in euthanasia, population control, and the phony "right" to abortion on demand, and yes, you can see it in the surrender of our national security.

It's all got to go. But how? Politics as usual will never get us there.

The cultural institutions have paved the road to this destruction of true freedom. We must make a U-turn on that road and take those institutions back. Electing the best politicians will never be enough. To turn this country around, freedom-loving revolutionaries must reclaim Hollywood, the foundations, the schools, academia, and, of course, the press.

The reason we must take back the press and all the other cultural institutions that have betrayed the American Dream is because they play such a big role in educating—or mis-educating—the public.

The Founding Fathers knew that even the best designed government wouldn't work if the people were not righteous, moral, and God-fearing—if they didn't love liberty and cherish it. A virtuous republic, they believed, required a virtuous people.

To practice self-government again, we must have a people capable of self-government. Today, our population has been so dumbed down by government schools, television, movies, and the sad state of the press establishment that we are getting the kind of government we deserve. We're moving toward tyranny.

I believe God has opened some doors for us recently—given us a chance to do our duty—with the advent of the New Media. We have had the opportunity to create new institutions that can challenge CNN, AP, Fox, Viacom, Disney, Universal—perhaps even the government schools and the factories of "higher education" that serve only the status quo.

The battlefield of ideas is being leveled.

But only when we create some serious competition within those powerful cultural institutions and begin taking them back with this potent new weapon of mass liberation, then and only then, will it really matter which of the major presidential candidates gets elected and which party controls Congress. Only then are we as a nation likely to make the political choices that matter. Only then will we be capable—and worthy—of self-government again.

In the meantime, we have a lot of work to do.

You may have heard about the survey in the former Great Britain earlier this year that revealed one in four Englishmen don't believe Prime Minister Winston Churchill actually existed.

They suspect he is a mythical character, rather than a historical one.

Likewise, they think historical figures such as Florence Nightingale, Sir Walter Raleigh, Mahatma Gandhi, and Cleopatra were also fictional personalities created for literature or films. On the other hand, they believe Sherlock Holmes was a real person.[1]

You can laugh about a survey like this, but I suspect we should all be very, very angry about it—at least the three-quarters of us who understand Churchill was not only a real guy but an important one in the history of Western civilization.

In fact, he wrote the book on Western civilization—the classic *A History of the English-Speaking Peoples*.

These results are even more stunning when you consider that about one-quarter of Britain's population was alive during Churchill's life.

But how would the rest of today's Brits know about this?

Who was supposed to tell them?

Where were they supposed to learn the basics of modern history?

For that matter, if Americans were polled, I suspect their performance would be even more humiliating. That's because education is in a shambles. I doubt very much if government-paid schoolteachers in either the United States or United Kingdom would know more than the general population. I wonder how many of them would know whether Winston Churchill was a real person.

That would be an interesting poll. But I won't hold my breath waiting for CNN or ABC or the *New York Times* to commission it any time soon.

They're too busy lobbying for more government spending and control over education. It seems you just can't get too much of a failed thing.

And "Failed," with a capital "F," is the only way to grade our modern, top-down, command-and-control, politically correct, centralized government mis-education system.

Having failed children and parents for twenty, thirty, forty years now, our very way of life is threatened as a result.

Surveys like this and my observations of the cultural decay surrounding us suggest to me we are in danger of losing our freedom.

Freedom isn't license.

Freedom is only attainable and sustainable with responsibility and knowledge.

Can anyone tell me with a straight face that we're as well-equipped for self-government as generations past?

Can anyone tell me we're wiser than our parents and grandparents?

Can anyone tell me our world is headed in a direction that is encouraging for our children and grandchildren?

We're headed into the gutter—into the sewer.

Western civilization is in real trouble. It is under attack. It is under siege.

It's about to go out not with a bang, but with a whimper.

No one is even fighting for it anymore. No one is championing it. No one is explaining what will replace it.

Please heed this warning: There is only one thing likely to fill the vacuum when it goes. It's called tyranny. You can call it other names—fascism, communism, socialism. They're all the same. They all mean people will be disempowered in favor of elites. After all, only the elites will be equipped intellectually to make the tough decisions.

That's the way it happens.

So, it's no laughing matter that one-quarter of Britons don't even realize Winston Churchill was a real person.

It's one of those signposts on the road to tyranny.

Blind ignorance isn't the only signpost. Blind immorality is another.

Abortion, homosexuality, the coarsening of our kids, attacks on Judeo-Christian values, the movement to destroy marriage, the seemingly intentional dumbing down of our children, moral relativism.

How is it that so much of what we once viewed as wrong is now perceived as right?

America has been sold a bill of goods.

It's not an accident. It's not chance. It's part of a deliberate plot—or, more precisely, a series of deliberate plots—to change the very character of America.

As you know by now, I've come to the conclusion that we've been breaking down the forces at work in our society in the wrong categories. We talk about liberals versus conservatives, Republicans versus Democrats, left versus right.

There are better ways to explain the battle.

It is first and foremost a spiritual war that is raging in America and throughout the world. Christians and Jews—who formed an uneasy partnership to build Western civilization and, ultimately, America—are under attack throughout the four corners of the world.

While jihadists and totalitarian socialists imprison, beat, and persecute us because we represent real freedom, here at home the attacks are more subtle, more clever.

Here, the battle is waged by those who love and cherish the American dream and those who resent it and want to transform it.

The American experiment in freedom is under siege by domestic enemies who seek to change the very definition of America—slowly, surely, inexorably. It's on the fast track today. But the process started a long time ago.

There is no way politics alone can get the job done.

Politicians do not lead. They follow. They do not stand up to the tremendous pressures applied by the cultural and political establishment. They bend. They compromise. They yield. It is unusual for a politician to place principle over personal ambition. And that's how the freedom stealers win battle after battle.

Gramsci figured that out. So did the Fabian socialists who are today so close to achieving their ultimate goals. They have thoroughly succeeded in sacking America's cultural institutions—and today, the political establishment is sitting there like an overripe plum waiting to be harvested.

That doesn't mean we give up. That doesn't mean we throw up our hands and declare defeat. That doesn't mean we surrender—not by a long shot. It means we fight harder—and smarter—than we have in a long, long time. It even means we learn from our enemies.

After all, it's not so much that we have lost ground in the cultural war. It's more like we never realized we were in a war to begin with. We lost by default.

Let me give you an example. From the 1930s through the mid-1960s, the churches, both Catholic and Protestant, wielded enormous clout in Hollywood, one of the most important cultural institutions in America. Clergy and laymen representing both branches of Christianity approved many scripts made into motion pictures by the major studios until 1968. At that time, the churches voluntarily relinquished this powerful influence they had over America's culture.

Why? Not because there was any pressure from the film industry. In fact, Hollywood moguls begged the churches to stay involved. They understood it was good for business. The involvement of the churches helped ensure that Hollywood produced films that would be well received by the vast mainstream audience. Left to their own devices, the studio heads understood they could easily lose touch—that artistic license could easily lead to licentiousness. Yet, I doubt any of them could have imagined how quickly the entertainment industry would plummet into the moral abyss.

The result? Just check it out at your local movie theater—or on prime-time television, for that matter. R-rated filth isn't limited to the big screen. What passed as risqué entertainment a few years ago on pay cable is now broadcast in the so-called family hour. Fewer people go to movies today than did after World War II. Only skyrocketing ticket prices, video rentals, and television distribution have kept the industry rolling in profits. But, is there anyone who doubts Hollywood would be better off, making higher profits, if it was still producing movies as it did in its Golden Age?

Why did the church abandon Hollywood? Because social activists who had penetrated the church as part of that long-range strategy devised by Gramsci engineered the move. There is simply no other rationale. At the time, the National Council of Churches, which oversaw the Protestant Film Office, claimed it could no longer afford to monitor scripts.

Today, the National Council of Churches is at the forefront of every statist social cause under the sun. Closing the film office was merely the first volley in a long war against freedom, personal responsibility, and self-government.

That's how the Culture War is waged. But, as Hollywood demonstrates, dropping out isn't the answer. The answer is for freedom-loving people to fight back on all fronts, to stop surrendering in the Culture War, to reclaim and redeem those lost cultural institutions. Even the mainline Christian churches have been lost.

While "conservatives" have been fighting a conventional political war for the last thirty years, the statists, the radical secularists, the socialists have been taking over the culture—the Ho Chi Minh trail to political power.

Is it any wonder we find it so difficult to govern ourselves when one of the central tenets of those cultural revolutionaries for the last seventy-five years has been the destruction of the whole notion of self-government?

I don't know if we'll be entirely successful—at least not without the direct hand of God. But I do know that we are commanded never to give in, never to yield to sin, never to surrender to the world. Our only choice, then, is to make every effort to reclaim ground in the Culture War. If our cultural institutions fell so easily to determined people with bad ideas, how much more success could we expect with a little persistence and good ideas like freedom, personal responsibility, and self-government?

I believe God will bless such a campaign. After all, the enemies of freedom are the enemies of God. They declared war on Him and the whole notion of a sovereign Supreme Being when they set out on their destructive path to empower the state as the ultimate authority. But God still sits on the throne. He's still in charge. His Spirit is far more powerful than any worldly forces.

It reminds me of the words of the revolutionary naval hero John Paul Jones as his foundering ship was besieged and bombarded by the British fleet. "I have not yet begun to fight," he said.

That's the spirit that will carry the day. That's the spirit that will be rewarded by God.

Do you know what the number one goal of Gramsci and his followers was—and remains today? It was to persuade people that God, if He exists at all, is basically irrelevant to the way we govern ourselves as individuals and as nations. Once faith and the personal morals they inspire become irrelevant, government becomes the supreme authority and only government force can prevent utter chaos.

There is only one thing that can right this listing American ship of state. The church needs to become re-engaged in our society. Pastors and rabbis need to speak out boldly and reassert responsibility in our culture. Faithful lay leaders need to put timidity and self-consciousness aside and talk about right and wrong.

We need to hear about sin again. We need to hear about eternal consequences for our actions. We need to hear about good and evil.

Jews and Christians alike need to reclaim the soul of this country.

There is something that each of us can do today besides wait for leadership, wait for someone else to act, wait for the situation to get even worse.

The Bible tells us in II Chronicles 7:14: "If my people, which are called by my name, shall humble themselves, and pray, and seek my face, and turn from their wicked ways; then will I hear from heaven, and will forgive their sin, and will heal their land."

Chapter Eleven

So What Are You Going to Do November 4?

THERE'S A CERTAIN significance to chapter eleven of this book about the 2008 election. I trust by now I have made the case that our political system is bankrupt. It's time to file for reorganization. The bills are coming due for years of abuse and corruption and bad business practices. It's time to start cleaning up the mess.

We can start doing that in a way that will make news and make history on November 4.

What are you going to do?

The reality is you do have a choice this November. But it's not between John McCain and Barack Obama. You can make a difference in the future of our country and vote for "none of the above."

That's the real historic choice we face this election year.

Are you going to start a bold new journey to freedom, justice, and morality the way our founders did 232 years ago? Or, are you going to drink deep of the Kool-Aid of conventional political wisdom and vote for the "lesser of two evils"?

Let me appeal one more time to your better angels.

More than two thousand years ago, Roman children trembled in fear at the thought of the Carthaginian military leader Hannibal attacking their city-state.

Hannibal finally reached the gates of Rome by moving his army across the Alps on elephants. But Rome didn't fall for another seven centuries.

It was a different enemy that felled the great empire—which had already been weakened from within by crumbling institutions.

Back in 1857, Lord Macaulay famously predicted a similar fate for the United States.

"Your Republic will be fearfully plundered and laid waste by barbarians in the 20th century as the Roman Empire was in the 5th," he said, "with the difference that the Huns and Vandals that ravaged the Roman Empire will have come from without and that your Huns and Vandals will have engendered within your own country by your own institutions."[1]

The twentieth century may have come and gone, but Lord Macaulay may be off by only a few years.

Indeed, there is an enemy within the gates of the American empire.

While we fight courageous and just causes on foreign soil against a tyrannical ideology that threatens the entire world, Americans are losing the ability to govern themselves at home.

We have forgotten what made us great.

We have forgotten how special American institutions are.

We have forgotten the principles set forth by our Founding Fathers that were so revolutionary.

As Daniel Webster explained, "Hold on, my friends, to the Constitution and to the Republic for which it stands. Miracles do not cluster, and what has happened once in 6,000 years, may not happen again. Hold on to the Constitution, for if the American Constitution should fail, there will be anarchy throughout the world."[2]

We have allowed the Constitution to fail.

We took it for granted.

We twisted it and subverted it.

We bent and shaped it to mean what we wanted it to mean.

We deliberately obscured the real intent and rewrote it in our minds.

We justified these distortions by rationalizing that it was a document written in another time.

We chipped away at it piece by piece until we were left with a country controlled by a central government in Washington with few of the limits placed upon it that the founders established.

We sat by idly while judicial oligarchs sat like high priests in black robes and issued rulings overturning the law of the land and the will of the people.

We accepted international treaties that cast our fate to the wind rather than maintain governments accountable to the people.

Worst of all, we allowed the notion that faith in a transcendent God was superfluous to the way we governed ourselves and our affairs. George Washington wrote:

> *Of all the dispositions and habits which lead to political prosperity, Religion and morality are indispensable supports. In vain would that man claim the tribute of Patriotism, who should labor to subvert these great Pillars of human happiness, these firmest props of the duties of Men and citizens. The mere Politician, equally with the pious man ought to respect and to cherish them. A volume could not trace all their connections with private and public felicity.*

> *Let it simply be asked where is the security for property, for reputation, for life, if the sense of religious obligation desert the oaths, which are the instruments of investigation in Courts of Justice? And let us with caution indulge the supposition, that morality can be maintained without religion. Whatever may be conceded to the influence of refined education on minds of peculiar structure, reason and experience both forbid us to expect the National morality can prevail in exclusion of religious principle.[3]*

He added: *"'Tis substantially true, that virtue or morality is a necessary spring of popular government. The rule indeed extends with more or less force to every species of free Government. Who that is a sincere friend to it, can look with indifference upon attempts to shake the foundation of the fabric?"*

And it was Thomas Jefferson who said, *"I tremble for my country when I reflect that God is just."*[4]

The foundation of our fabric has been shaken, indeed, in recent years. Freedom is unknowable and unachievable apart from the promises of God.

Americans have become their own worst enemy.

Certainly there are external foes to be feared and triumphed over. Certainly there are foreign threats. Certainly we live in a dangerous period of history—even if our people were unified and strong.

But we are not unified and strong. We no longer know who we are or what sets us apart.

And that has rendered America more vulnerable to subversion from within than to force from without.

But it's not too late for America, is it?

What do you suppose would happen if a significant number of us reoriented the way we think about the issues of the day, became better informed, and emboldened ourselves with the kind of courage and passion our founders had in establishing this great nation?

I believe that effort would be blessed by God. Indeed, God sent twelve men out to change the world. Certainly a few million of us could change America.

Let's take the first baby step in that direction November 4 by voting for "none of the above." Remember, this is not a "non-vote." If someone tries to tell you that, please explain you are casting the most important and powerful vote of your life when you vote for someone other than Barack Obama or John McCain. You are voting against business as usual. You are voting against two evils. You are voting against non-choices. You are voting for freedom, justice, and the Constitution of the United States.

Is there a more principled vote to be cast this year or any other?

There's no consensus in America today for either of these two major-party candidates. And there's a reason for that. They are not speaking to us. They are not addressing the root problems in America today. Neither of these candidates is saying what I want to hear from a candidate for president in 2008. Neither is addressing the eternal truths or the great ideas. So what are these big ideas and eternal truths?

If I were running for president this year, my campaign stump speech would incorporate the following:

- The day I take office, I would declare a national day of prayer and fasting for the future of our country. We live in dangerous times—with challenges at home and abroad. I want to ensure that we make every effort to beseech the God of the universe to bestow His blessings and favor upon us. This would be in the great tradition of other early American presidents who recognized we must humble ourselves before the Almighty. And, you know what? I would mean it.

- On my second day in office, while breaking my fast that morning, I would begin implementing my bully-pulpit plan to dismantle the Internal Revenue Service and eliminate the income tax forevermore. How do you think that would play in Peoria?

- On my third day in office, I would not just begin my fight against all unconstitutional efforts to restrict firearms in America, I would urge Americans to arm themselves—because it's the right thing to do. There would be no better anti-crime program, no better antiterrorist program, and no better anti-tyranny program than a heavily armed civilian population.

- On my fourth day in office, I would make sure the executive branch of government was doing everything in its power to erect the border fence. I would explain that there would be no discussion by the White House about any amnesty plans or guest worker programs until the border fence was complete and Americans had confidence that we knew who was entering our country.

- On the fifth day, we'd begin exploring all the ways we could enforce our immigration policies inside our borders—with employer sanctions and attacking sanctuary cities and challenging court rulings on anchor babies and taking the fight to illegal alien gangs like MS-13.

- On the sixth day, I'd talk directly to the American people, explaining how they'd been lied to, deceived into believing government was their friend. I'd tell them their hope is in God, as well as freedom, self-reliance, and personal responsibility.

- On the seventh day, I would rest.

- On the eighth day, I'd begin my assault on all the wealth redistribution programs of the federal government. I might not be able to eliminate them all—but I'd give it my best shot.

- On the ninth day, I'd ask Ruth Bader Ginsburg to retire from her seat on the Supreme Court so I could nominate a strict constructionist justice who would vote to

overturn *Roe v. Wade*, that illegitimate piece of
judicial activist legislation.

Maybe you like my ideas; maybe you have your own set of
priorities. But the point is we need radical actions to get our
country back on a constitutional footing. McCain and Obama
will only take us radically in the other direction.

You'll hear a lot about "change" from the two major-party
candidates between now and November 4.

"Do you want change?" they'll ask—waiting for applause.

"Are you ready for change?" they'll ask—knowing it is
exactly what Americans fundamentally want.

"It's time for change in America," they'll say—meaning,"T
rust me to do whatever I want with your money and the
power you give me."

Do you know why these politicians are always asking you
if you want change?

Because that's what they both are going to leave in your
pocket when elected.

Hillary Clinton was more candid in one of her campaign
stops during the Democratic primaries. She let this one slip out:
"I have a million ideas. The country can't afford them all."[5]

She was right—but not just about her plans. We can't
afford either one of the last two men standing for the major
parties. They both want to spend your money for programs
and missions unauthorized by the Constitution.

By this point you may be wondering why anyone in their
right mind would consider voting for McCain or Obama. Yet,
you and I both know they will receive far more votes than any
third-party or independent candidate in 2008. That's the sad
reality. But under my "none of the above" plan, we don't have
to defeat them. We don't have to have victory for a dark-horse
independent to make our point. We just have to make a good
showing—one that will encourage real competition in the
political marketplace.

Over the last thirty years or so, the American people have been intentionally dumbed down. You may not believe it, but it's a deliberate effort to make us dumber than our parents, grandparents, and great-grandparents.

That's why approximately 90 percent of Americans are ready to gulp the Kool-Aid and vote for Barack Obama or John McCain to be the next president.

The good news, of course, is that in 2008, there will be more disaffection for the two major-party candidates than ever before.

Remember, we will never get better candidates if we accept lesser candidates. It's simple market politics, as I have explained earlier in this book. Your vote in 2008, therefore, is about more than the results of the 2008 election. It will affect future choices and future elections. Remember, also, the central reason for not voting for the two major candidates is because they betray the Constitution of the United States. Is it too much to ask that presidential candidates understand, uphold, and revere the Constitution? I believe it is an absolute minimal standard. Tell me why I am wrong, please! This should be a prerequisite of every American.

As voters, we need to raise our standards. Otherwise, we will get candidates whose standards reflect the lowest common denominator—not the ideals of life, liberty, and pursuit of happiness.

If politicians want our votes to empower themselves, they should have to earn them.

What is so hard to understand about that?

It is easier to think these thoughts than to practice them in the real world. It is easier to say these things than to live them. It is easier to write these words than to carry them out.

Here are some thoughts to keep you strong, to keep you convinced of your position, to help you avoid the temptations you will encounter as candidates and parties call you incessantly and bombard you with commercial messages in the coming days and weeks.

Why "none of the above"?

It's about the Constitution, stupid.

That's what you can tell those telemarketers when they call.

That's what you can write back on those Republican and Democratic Party fundraising letters.

It's about the Constitution, stupid.

Forty-eight days before Election Day comes a date few of us have marked on our calendars. But, as Americans, we all should be commemorating it. September 17 is Constitution Day. I want you to take note of that right now. It was 221 years ago the Constitutional Convention, meeting in Philadelphia for four months, agreed on the final draft of this special, inspired document and submitted it to the several states for ratification.

It was ratified June 21, 1788, when New Hampshire approved it as the ninth state. Congress, acting under the Articles of Confederation, declared the Constitution the law of the land March 4, 1789.

By general assent and resolution of the Congress, September 17 has been designated as Constitution Day ever since—designated, but not necessarily acknowledged or observed.

In the twenty-first century, we celebrate many holidays in America—Independence Day, presidential birthdays, Veterans Day, Memorial Day. Yet, no one even acknowledges Constitution Day anymore. That's tragic. I also believe it is intentional. I don't believe politicians want Americans thinking about the Constitution. Why? Because it strictly limits their power over you!

America has forgotten the two concepts that made her special as a nation—two unique factors that set her apart from the world from the start.

First, the Founding Fathers wrote a Constitution that strictly limited the role of the federal government in the lives of Americans. The idea that Washington had some role in education, redistribution of wealth, setting minimum wage requirements, nationalizing millions of acres of land, taxing income and subsidizing government-approved artists would have been anathema to the men who fought so valiantly for freedom against an overreaching foreign tyranny—if they could have even imagined such abuses.

Second, the framers of that Constitution spoke eloquently about the fact that only a moral people—a nation of godly people with common spiritual and social values—were capable of self-government. They could not have envisioned the depths of depravity, licentiousness, and vice to which our society has fallen—yet they warned about it.

Our current debates about social and government policy seem disconnected from these two critical foundations of the American republic. Politicians will never solve the problems facing the country without acknowledging these two essential precepts.

In fact, I'll go further. Politicians will never solve our problems. Period. The more government tries to do, the worse things get.

And that's the beauty of the Constitution. It strictly limits what government can do. The trouble is that Americans have forgotten this. They've been dumbed down by government schools and a government-media complex to believe that Uncle Sam is there to solve all their problems—from how much they get paid to what they spend on healthcare, to how they should raise their own children.

We honor the flag in America, but not the Constitution. The flag is a mere symbol. The Constitution is the real thing. We should revere it, and, more importantly, live under it.

Why do we salute the flag and not the Constitution? The Constitution is every bit as symbolic as the flag, but it is much more—a guidepost to maintaining (or now, perhaps, to recovering) America's freedom. But it can serve that function only if we as a nation abide by it, pay heed to it, live by its code and its spirit.

Which symbol is really worth dying for? The flag is not my pick. After all, it is just a symbol. Symbols, of course, are important. But the Constitution is more. It is both symbol and substance. And its substance is being desecrated by some of those so piously concerned about the symbolic desecration of the flag.

A few years ago, a public opinion survey found that less than half of American adults would vote for the Constitution if it were on the ballot today. To that, I say, thank God there is no requirement for a referendum on the Constitution. Another poll showed close to half of Americans don't believe in the basic First Amendment guarantees of freedom of speech, assembly, religion, and the press.

So, there you see it. The Constitution is being desecrated before our eyes. Here in one document are the guiding principles of our nation succinctly and clearly stated. The Constitution, coupled with the Declaration of Independence, represents more of a national creed than a simple founding document for the nation.

Shouldn't it be our minimal standard for presidential candidates, who, upon taking office, swear an oath to uphold and defend it?

If even 10 percent of Americans would take this principle seriously in the 2008 election, it would shake up the political system in a profound and permanent way. It would change the political dynamic in the United States. It would be the first step to applying market forces to our political choices.

This election year can be a turning point in American history.

It won't be if Americans choose the lesser of two evils between the two front-running major-party candidates.

But let's examine the possibilities if Americans heed my recommendation and vote for "none of the above"—writing in their protest vote or lodging one with a third-party candidate of their choice.

In April of this year, one in four Hillary Clinton supporters said they would not vote for Barack Obama if he became the nominee. Keep in mind she won more votes throughout the Democratic primaries than he did.

Obama could still conceivably win, but the Democratic presidential nominee would have to do it with a low turnout of Democratic voters. That's a good thing.

There is little excitement being generated among Republican voters for their standard bearer this year. Even Rush Limbaugh, probably the most important Republican voice in the country, has been harshly critical of McCain.

There are other factors in play that could make this a historic year for low turnout for the major parties. There has never been a presidential election in which two major-party nominees were both sitting senators. It is extremely rare that a sitting U.S. senator wins the race. This year, the two major-party candidates are sitting U.S. senators. Traditionally, the American people show understanding that legislators do not necessarily have the qualifications for the executive position of president. In this case, both candidates have nothing in their résumés resembling the kind of executive experience that would qualify them for the job.

Despite their protests of such an assertion, the reality is there is little policy difference between them. In fact, McCain, Obama, and Hillary Clinton have co-sponsored eighty-six bills together since 2005.

There has never been an age gap so large between the two major-party candidates for president. McCain is seventy. Obama is forty-six. There are questions being raised about McCain being too old and questions being raised about Obama being too young.

There is much disaffection this year for both parties and for both candidates. This is a good thing. Add to this reality a budding campaign to withhold votes from both major-party candidates—the purpose of this book—and you have the makings of a historic turning point in American political history.

It is with this in mind that your non-vote could have far more impact than a vote for McCain or Obama.

This is the year to send the major parties a message. This is the year to open the possibilities for more competition in our political marketplace. This is the year to break the hammerlock of control the two, corrupt, out-of-touch major political parties have over the American people and public policy.

This could be the most exciting year ever to go to the polls and vote—for "none of the above."

It's time to get radical.

It's time to get out into the streets.

It's time to emulate our Founding Fathers.

It's time to take America back.

Start by voting for "none of the above" in 2008.

NOTES

CHAPTER ONE NOTES

1. *YourDictionary.com*, http://www.yourdictionary.com/hysteria.

2. Bill Blakemore, "'Schwarzenator' vs. Bush: Global Warming Debate Heats Up," *ABC News*, August 30, 2006, http://abcnews.go.com/US/GlobalWarming/Story?id=2374968&page=1.

3. Jack Kemp, "Al Gore's Legacy of Hypocrisy," *American Thinker*, March 1, 2007. Also see Peter Schweizer, "Gore isn't quite as green as he's led the world to believe," *USA Today*, December 7, 2006.

4. *WorldNetDaily*, "Gore's 'carbon offsets' paid to firm he owns," March 2, 2007, http://www.worldnetdaily.com/news/article.asp?ARTICLE_ID=54528.

5. Thomas Jefferson, "Report of the Commissioners for the University of Virginia," August 4, 1818, Cited in Yarborough, Jean M., *The Essential Jefferson* (Indianapolis, IN: Hackett Publishing, 2006) 66-67.

6. *CBS News*, "911 Operators Disciplined After Woman On Hold Dies," February 13, 2008, http://cbs3.com/national/Brenda.Orr.Fire.2.653337.html.

7. Ibid.

8. *Webster's New World Dictionary*, http://www.yourdictionary.com/colony.

CHAPTER TWO NOTES

1. Phillip Elliot, "Obama Gets Warning from Friendly Voter," *Associated Press*, August 14, 2007, http://www.washingtonpost.com/wp-dyn/content/article/2007/08/14/AR2007081400812.html.

2. Nedra Picker, "Fact Check: Obama on Afghanistan," *Associated Press*, August 14, 2007, http://www.washingtonpost.com/wp-dyn/content/article/2007/08/14/AR2007081400950_pf.html.

3. *WorldNetDaily*, "Obama calls Hazleton ruling 'a victory for all Americans'", July 29, 2007, http://www.worldnetdaily.com/news/article.asp?ARTICLE_ID=56904.

4. Ibid.

5. Ibid.

6. Cliff Kinkaid and Herbert Romerstein, "Communism in Hawaii and the Obama Connection" (Special Report), America's Survival, Inc., http://www.usasurvival.org/docs/hawaii-obama.pdf.

7. Cliff Kinkaid and Herbert Romerstein, "Communism in Chicago and the Obama Connection" (Special Report), America's Survival, Inc., http://www.usasurvival.org/docs/chicago-obama.pdf.

8. Ibid.

9. Ibid.

10. Ibid.

11. *WorldNetDaily*, "Che flag sends 'disturbing' message about Obama," February 13, 2008, http://www.wnd.com/index.php?fa=PAGE.view&pageId=56293.

12. *Investor's Business Daily*, "Barack Guevara," February 12, 2008, http://www.ibdeditorials.com/IBDArticles.aspx?id=287712495807374.

13. All information regarding Che Guevara in the previous paragraphs is cited in Joseph Farah, "Barack Che Guevera:" a *WorldNetDaily* "Between the Lines" exclusive commentary, *WorldNetDaily*, February 14, 2008, http://www.worldnetdaily.com/index.php?pageId=56303.

14. Dinita Smith, "No Regrets for a Love Of Explosives; In a Memoir of Sorts, a War Protester Talks of Life With the Weathermen," *New York Times*, September 11, 2001, http://query.nytimes.com/gst/fullpage.html?res=9F02E1DE1438F932A2575AC0A9679C8B63&sec=&spon=&pagewanted=all.

15. Ibid.

16. Ibid.

17. Dinita Smith, "No Regrets for a Love Of Explosives; In a Memoir of Sorts, a War Protester Talks of Life With the Weathermen," *New York Times*, September 11, 2001, http://query.nytimes.com/gst/fullpage.html?res=9F02E1DE1438F932A2575AC0A9679C8B63&sec=&spon=&pagewanted=all

18. John M. Fountain, "Northwestern Alumni to End Donations if Ex-Radical Stays," *New York Times*, November 4, 2001, http://query.nytimes.com/gst/fullpage.html?res=9D01E0DA1739F937A35752C1A9679C8B63&scp=125&sq=Bill+Ayers&st=nyt.

19. Ibid. Also see Daniel J. Wakin, "Quieter Lives for 60's Militants, but Intensity of Beliefs hasn't Faded," *New York Times*, August 24, 2003, http://query.nytimes.com/gst/fullpage.html?res=9F04E4DE1539F937A1575BC0A9659C8B63&scp=147&sq=Bill+Ayers&st=nyt.

20. John Kass, "Underground links likely to resurface for Obama," *Chicago Tribune*, April 23, 2008, http://www.chicagotribune.com/news/columnists/chi-kass-23-apr23,1,4967065.column.

21. http://en.wikipedia.org/wiki/The_Audacity_of_Hope

22. *New York Times*, "Obama's 2006 Speech on Faith and Politics," June 28, 2008, http://www.nytimes.com/2006/06/28/us/politics/2006obamaspeech.html?pagewanted=2&ref=politics.

23. Ibid.

24. Ibid.

25. Ibid.

26. Cited in Brian Ross and Rehab El-Buri, "Obama's Pastor: God Damn America, U.S. to Blame for 9/11," *ABC News*, March 13, 2008, http://abcnews.go.com/Blotter/Story?id=4443788.

27. Ibid.

28. Cited in Ronald Kessler, "Obama Minister's Hatred of America," Washington Insider with Ronald Kessler, *Newsmax*, March 6, 2008, http://www.newsmax.com/kessler/obama_minister_wright/2008/03/06/78440.html.

29. Ibid.

30. Ibid.

31. Ibid.

32. Brian Ross and Rehab El-Buri, "Obama's Pastor: God Damn America, U.S. to Blame for 9/11," *ABC News*, March 13, 2008, http://abcnews.go.com/Blotter/Story?id=4443788.

33. The video and transcript of Michelle Obama's infamous statement can be found online here: http://www.breitbart.tv/html/49244.html.

34. Lauren Collins, "The Other Obama," *The New Yorker*, March 10, 2008, http://www.newyorker.com/reporting/2008/03/10/080310fa_fact_collins?curr entPage=1.

35. Ibid.

36. Ibid.

37. Ibid.

38. Barack Obama, "Remarks of Senator Barack Obama: 'A More Perfect Union,'" March 18, 2008, http://www.barackobama.com/2008/03/18/ remarks_of_senator_barack_obam_53.php.

39. Barack Obama, interview with *The Morning Show* on 610 AM in Philadelphia, March 20, 2008, transcript accessed at http://www.glennbeck.com/content/articles/article/198/7636/.

40. Jennifer Parker and Olivia Sterns, "Ferraro Steps Down from Clinton Campaign," *ABC News*, March 12, 2008, http://abcnews.go.com/GMA/ Vote2008/story?id=4435376.

41. Barack Obama, "The Audacity of Hope," 2004 Democratic National Convention Keynote Address, July 27, 2004, accessed at http://www.americanrhetoric.com/speeches/convention2004/barackobama 2004dnc.htm.

42. CNN, "Democratic Candidates Compassion Forum," April 13, 2008, transcript accessed at http://transcripts.cnn.com/TRANSCRIPTS/0804/13/ se.01.html.

43. Michael Gerson, "Obama's Abortion Extremism," *Washington Post*, April 2, 2008, A19, http://www.washingtonpost.com/wp-dyn/content/article/2008/04/01/AR2008040102197.html.

44. David Brody, "Obama Says He Doesn't Want His Daughters Punished with a Baby," CBN News, March 31, 2008, http://www.cbn.com/cbnnews/348569.aspx.

45. *New York Times*, "The Democratic Debate in Cleveland," February 26, 2008, transcript accessed at http://www.nytimes.com/2008/02/26/us/politics/26text-debate.html?pagewanted=21.

46. Frank Main, "Obama's Rezko Ties go Deeper than Land Deal," *Chicago Sun-Times*, December 23, 2006, http://www.suntimes.com/news/politics/184540,122306obama.article.

CHAPTER THREE NOTES

1. Public Papers and Addresses of the Presidents of the United States: John F. Kennedy, 1962 (Washington: U.S. Government Printing Office, 1963), pp. 879-80. See also Economic Report of the President, 1963 (Washington: U.S. Government Printing Office, 1963), p. xiv.

2. Cited in William J. Federer, *The Interesting History of Income Tax* (St. Louis, MO: Americsearch, 2004), 105.

3. Ibid., 107.

4. Ibid., 157.

5. Walter Williams, "Rights vs. Wishes," *Capitalism Magazine*, October 27, 2002, http://www.capmag.com/article.asp?ID=2005.

6. http://www.nrlc.org/abortion/facts/abortionstats.html.

7. *NY Times*, "Barack Obama's March 4 Speech," March 4, 2008, http://www.nytimes.com/2008/03/04/us/politics/04text-obama.html.

8. Barack Obama, "The Audacity of Hope," 2004 Democratic National Convention Keynote Address, July 27, 2004, accessed at

http://www.americanrhetoric.com/speeches/convention2004/barackobam
a2004dnc.htm.

9. *Power Line*, "Al of Arabia," February 13, 2006,
http://www.powerlineblog.com/archives/013130.php.

10. Oliver Burkeman, "Bill Clinton: Hillary wants me to restore image of
U.S.," *Guardian*, October 5, 2007, http://www.guardian.co.uk/world/2007/oct/
05/topstories3.usa.

11. CBS News, "Jimmy Carter Slams Iraq War," July 30, 2005,
http://www.cbsnews.com/stories/2005/07/30/politics/main712910.shtml.

12. *Guardian.co.uk*, "Jimmy Carter Wins Nobel Peace Prize," October 11,
2002, http://www.guardian.co.uk/world/2002/oct/11/2.

13. MSNBC, "Democratic Debate Transcript," October 30, 2007,
Transcript accessed at http://www.msnbc.msn.com/id/21528787/page/22/.

14. US Newswire, "DNC Chairman Howard Dean Recognizes the 33rd
Anniversary of *Roe vs. Wade*," January 23, 2006, http://findarticles.com/
p/articles/mi_hb5554/is_200601/ai_n21865787.

15. *Telegraph.co.uk*, "Smoker Refused Operation on Broken Ankle,"
September 17, 2007, http://www.telegraph.co.uk/news/worldnews/1563108/
Smoker-refused-operation-on-broken-ankle.html#continue.

16. Democratic Debate Transcript, September 26, 2007, Dartmouth
College, MSNBC, Transcript accessed at http://www.msnbc.msn.com/id/
21327206/page/11/.

17. Dan Balz and Chris Cillizza, "Clyburn: Positive Report By Petraeus
Could Split House Democrats On War," *Washington Post*, July 30, 2007.

18. Kate Phillips, "Kennedy: 'George Bush's Vietnam'," *The Caucus: New
York Times Political Blog*, January 9, 2007, http://thecaucus.blogs.nytimes.com/
2007/01/09/kennedy-george-bushs-vietnam/.

19. http://www.opensecrets.org/pfds/pfd2007/N00007360_2007.pdf.

20. *Investor's Business Daily*, "Nancy Pelosi's Sour Grapes," October 31,
2006, http://www.investors.com/editorial/editorialcontent.asp?secid=

1501&status=article&id=247191278714751.

21. Peter Schweizer, *Do As I Say (Not As I Do)* (New York: Broadway, 2006).

22. *WorldNetDaily*, "Pelosi leader of 'Progressive Caucus,'" November 11, 2002, http://www.worldnetdaily.com/news/article.asp?ARTICLE_ID=29612. Also see Joseph Farah, "Congress' Red Army caucus, *WorldNetDaily*, July 28, 1998, http://www.worldnetdaily.com/news/article.asp?ARTICLE_ID=14542.

23. Cited in Joseph Farah, "Nancy Pelosi: 'Caviar Commie," *WorldNetDaily*, November 6, 2006, http://www.worldnetdaily.com/news/article.asp?ARTICLE_ID=52798.

24. Ibid.

CHAPTER FOUR NOTES

1. Jonathan Chait, "Maverick vs. Iceman," *New Republic*, February 10, 2008, http://www.tnr.com/politics/story.html?id=4a65fb2f-7752-493f-a8d3-7fa4aa5e55d0.

2. Elisabeth Bumiller, "McCain's Vote In 2000 is Revived in a Ruckus," *New York Times*, May 9, 2008, http://www.nytimes.com/2008/05/09/us/politics/09huffington.html.

3. Judicial Watch, "Radical Chicano Group Gets Millions in Earmarks," May 6, 2008, http://www.judicialwatch.org/blog/radical-chicano-group-gets-millions-earmarks.

4. Michelle Malkin, "Top 10 reasons McCain should repudiate the National Council of La Raza," May 6, 2008, *MichelleMalkin.com*, http://michellemalkin.com/2008/05/06/top-10-reasons-mccain-should-repudiate-the-national-council-of-la-raza/.

5. Brian Ross, Avni Patel, and Rehab El-Buri, "McCain Pastor: Islam Is a 'Conspiracy of Spiritual Evil,' May 22, 2008, ABC News, http://abcnews.go.com/Blotter/story?id=4905624.

6. Ibid.

7. Ibid.

8. American Civil Liberties Union, "Mr. Smith Goes to Washington.com: How a Small-Town Internet Speaker Tripped Over Campaign Finance Regulations," October 13, 1999, http://www.aclu.org/votingrights/cfr/

12963prs19991013.html.

9. Ibid.

10. Jerome Corsi, "John McCain funded by Soros since 2001," *WorldNetDaily*, February 12, 2008, http://www.worldnetdaily.com/index. php?fa=PAGE.view&pageId=56177.

11. Associated Press, "McCain holds town hall meeting at Rice," February 29, 2008, http://abclocal.go.com/ktrk/story?section=news/politics& id=5987016.

12. Ibid.

13. Ibid.

14. Kim Yon-se, "34 Percent of Army Cadets Regard US as Main Enemy," *Korea Times*, April 6, 2008, http://www.koreatimes.co.kr/www/ news/nation/2008/04/116_22029.html.

15. Dan Nowicki, "A McCain cabinet could bear shades of Teddy Roosevelt," *Arizona Republic*, February 19, 2008.

16. Jonathan Singer, "John Kerry: McCain Approached Me About Joining Dem Ticket in 2004," *Direct Democracy*, April 3, 2007, http://www.mydd.com/story/2007/4/3/11936/97033.

CHAPTER FIVE NOTES

1. *WorldNetDaily*, "Voinovich Self-Destructs on Hannity," June 27, 2007, http://www.wnd.com/news/article.asp?ARTICLE_ID=56414.

2. Ronald Reagan, Message to the Senate Returning without Approval the Fairness in Broadcasting Bill, June 19, 1987, accessed at http://www.reagan.utexas.edu/archives/speeches/1987/061987h.htm.

3. *Washington Post*, July 30, 2002, http://findarticles.com/p/articles/ mi_qa3827/is_200208/ai_n9097822.

CHAPTER SEVEN NOTES

NOTES

1. Richard Land, "'Lesser Evil', or 'Lesser Good'?" *Baptist Press*, October 3, 2007, http://www.bpnews.net/printerfriendly.asp?ID=26547.

2. Ibid.

CHAPTER EIGHT NOTES

1. Attributed to Marcus Tullius Cicero, *Congressional Record*, April 25, 1968, vol. 114, p. 10635.

2. http://www.pbs.org/wgbh/pages/frontline/endgame/view/.

CHAPTER NINE NOTES

1. Proverbs 29:18 (King James Version).

2. http://en.wikipedia.org/wiki/Edmund_Burke.

3. http://www.reaganlibrary.com/reagan/speeches/rendezvous.asp.

CHAPTER TEN NOTES

1. *Financial Express*, "Gandhi-Churchill 'myth,' Sherlock Real for Britons," February 4, 2008, http://www.financialexpress.com/news/Gandhi-Churchill-myth-Sherlock-real-for-Britons/268868/

CHAPTER ELEVEN NOTES

1. Cited in Joseph Farah, "Hannibal is inside the gates," *WorldNetDaily*, May 11, 2004, http://www.worldnetdaily.com/news/article.asp?ARTICLE_ID=38436.

2. Ibid.

3. George Washington, "Farewell Address," 1796, accessed at http://www.yale.edu/lawweb/avalon/washing.htm.

4. http://www.brainyquote.com/quotes/quotes/t/q157225.html

5. Marcella Bombardieri, "Clinton vows to check executive power," *Boston Globe*, October 11, 2007.